Alive in Christ

Alive in Christ

Ephesians simply explained

Stuart Olyott

 EVANGELICAL PRESS

EVANGELICAL PRESS
Faverdale North, Darlington, DL3 0PH, England

e-mail: sales@evangelicalpress.org

Evangelical Press USA
P. O. Box 825, Webster, New York 14580, USA

e-mail: usa.sales@evangelicalpress.org

web: http://www.evangelicalpress.org

First published 1994
Reprinted 2008, 2010

British Library Cataloguing in Publication Data available

ISBN 13 978 085234 315 9   ISBN 0 85234 315 9

Printed and bound in Great Britain by the MPG Books Group

Contents

Preface

When a Christian begins to understand Paul's epistle to the Ephesians, something wonderful happens to his spiritual life. Realizing how rich he is in Christ, he becomes filled with thankfulness and joy. He never envies non-Christians again. He sees what it means to live as a Christian in today's world. He becomes stable in his doctrinal understanding. In short, Ephesians produces exactly the sort of Christians we most need.

That is why this short commentary has been written. It is for those who want to begin to understand Paul's great letter. More advanced believers may also find some spiritual refreshment here, but they must not expect to discover anything new. There is not an original thought anywhere. Chapter 3, for example, owes a great deal to *The grace of God in the gospel* (Cheeseman, Gardner, Sadgrove and Wright), published by the Banner of Truth Trust in 1972.

May a fresh reading of Ephesians help all of us to 'grow up in all things into him who is the head — Christ'! (Eph. 4:15).

Stuart Olyott
Belvidere Road Church
Liverpool
March 1994

1.
Why study Ephesians?

Please read Ephesians 1:1-6

There is no better way to introduce Paul's letter to the Ephesians than to let it speak for itself. Let's read the first six verses of the book and, with them open before us, ask two questions: why we should bother, and whether these verses tell us much about spiritual blessings.

Why bother?

Why should we bother to study this letter at all? What is so special about it? These first verses give us four good reasons for spending time on this venture.

1. Because of who it is from

It is from **'Paul, an apostle of Jesus Christ by the will of God'**. Early in the first century there lived in Galilee a Jewish family of some note. In the Roman empire, most Jewish people were not considered worthy of much respect. This family was different because its members were Roman citizens — a privilege which, somewhere along the line, had been conferred on it, or had been bought.

This respected and prosperous family moved from Galilee to Asia Minor and settled in the seaport and commercial centre of Tarsus. It was there that a boy was born to them. He was born free, a Roman citizen from birth. Brought up in the strictest Jewish traditions and culture, educated as a Pharisee, he went to Jerusalem to pursue his higher studies under Gamaliel, the most celebrated Jewish teacher of his day. It must have been clear to all that this young man was destined to rise to the heights of influence in Jewish society. His family and religious credentials were impeccable. He was a man of means. He had received an education unparalleled by that of most of his peers and friends.

And so it proved to be. Before long the young Pharisee from Tarsus was enjoying a status out of all proportion to his age and experience. His rise to prominence was meteoric. The door of the Jewish supreme council, the Sanhedrin, duly opened to him and there he took his seat. The name of the young man was on every Jewish lip. He was the most promising Jew of his time. He epitomized all that first-century Judaism stood for. He had actually become what every young Jew wanted to be.

As the gospel spread in the early world, this young man of status became its most severe opponent. He made full use of his enormous influence to secure official authority to put down Christians and to free Palestine from their troublesome teachings. It was while he was madly pursuing them to the northern city of Damascus that a most remarkable thing happened to him. At noon, when the oriental sun was at its brightest, he was confronted by a light which was even brighter. Struck to the ground and blinded, he was arrested by Jesus Christ, the living Son of God. 'Rise and stand on your feet', he said, 'for I have appeared to you for this purpose, to make you a minister and a witness both of the things which you have seen and of the things which I will yet reveal to you. I will deliver you from the Jewish people, as well as from the Gentiles, to whom I now send you, to open their eyes, to turn them from darkness to light, and from the power of Satan to God, that they may receive forgiveness of sins and an inheritance among those who are sanctified by faith in me' (Acts 26:16-18).

So it was that the arrogant pinnacle of Jewish society, staggering, blinded and humbled, was told by the Lord of glory that he was to be his messenger to the Gentiles. He was personally commissioned to the task by Christ himself. Did he wonder if he was having hallucinations? Did he doubt that the vision was real? If so, these doubts were soon to be demolished. In nearby Damascus, the Lord was now to speak to somebody else. His word came to Ananias, who had been a Christian for some time, telling him that he was going to meet Saul of Tarsus when he came into the city. "'Lord," said Ananias, "I have heard from many about this man, how much harm he has done to your saints in Jerusalem. And here he has authority from the chief priests to bind all who call on your name."

'But the Lord said to him, "Go, for he is a chosen vessel of mine to bear my name before Gentiles, kings, and the children of Israel. For I will show him how many things he must suffer for my name's sake." And Ananias went his way and entered the house; and laying his hands on him he said, "Brother Saul, the Lord Jesus, who appeared to you on the road as you came, has sent me that you may receive your sight and be filled with the Holy Spirit"' (Acts 9:13-17). 'Then he said, "The God of our fathers has chosen you that you should know his will, and see the Just One, and hear the voice of his mouth. For you will be his witness to all men of what you have seen and heard"' (Acts 22:14-15).

In this way it was confirmed to Paul that he had not been imagining things. From Ananias' mouth, too, he heard that he had been chosen by Christ and had been given the special responsibility of proclaiming the truth of the gospel to the Gentiles. Quite soon, this fact was recognized generally by the churches, as well as by the other apostles.

This is why Paul opens up his letter to the Ephesians as he does: 'Paul, an apostle of Jesus Christ by the will of God'. He had been personally commissioned by the risen Christ to be an authoritative teacher of his gospel. And why was this? Because it was God's will that it should be so. There was no explanation, except that 'it pleased God' (Gal. 1:15).

In the years between his conversion and writing to the Ephesians, the apostle Paul was not 'disobedient to the heavenly vision, but declared first to those in Damascus and in Jerusalem, and throughout all the region of Judea, and then to the Gentiles, that they should repent, turn to God, and do works befitting repentance' (Acts 26:19-20). He went to Tarsus and preached for ten years in that one town, and in the region around. At Barnabas' request he taught the infant church in Syrian Antioch for a year. Sent out with Barnabas from that church, he preached throughout southern Asia Minor before returning to Antioch. On a second missionary journey, he went throughout Asia Minor again, and then into Europe. On a third journey he was based in Ephesus for three years, where he witnessed a widespread turning to the faith. The city became the base for operations by which the gospel was disseminated in Asia Minor, and over the water in Macedonia and Greece. It was on a return visit to Jerusalem that he was arrested, and eventually realized his lifelong ambition to preach the gospel in Rome.

But Paul arrived in Rome as a prisoner. It was in A.D. 62, while still a prisoner there, that he penned the words we are now reading. Perhaps chained to a Roman soldier, and with very few companions around him, he wrote letters — one to his friend Philemon, one to the Colossians, one to the Philippians, and this one, to be read by the Christians at Ephesus.

And we are reading it too. How privileged we are! We have in our hands a letter from such a man of God as this. Paul was the greatest theologian who has ever lived. But he was not an armchair theologian, hidden away in his ivory tower, and afraid to venture into the world. Not at all! He was a compassionate and courageous soul-winner, a missionary, an evangelist. More important than all that, he was the man personally commissioned by the resurrected Christ to teach the faith to the Gentiles. He knew Christ's mind and taught with his authority. Clearly it is more than worth the effort to find out what he has to say in this letter.

2. Because of the people to whom it is addressed

This letter is **'to the saints who are in Ephesus, and faithful in Christ Jesus'**.

The letter to the Ephesians is, then, addressed to a local church. Ephesus, while not the capital, was the first city of the Roman province of Asia. As far as international trade was concerned, it was one of the three most important cities of the early world, forming a triangle with Alexandria in Egypt and Antioch in Syria. An important port, it was a very cosmopolitan community. It was also a famous centre for the arts, being a well-known haven for philosophers, poets, artists and orators of all descriptions. Only Corinth, just across the Aegean Sea, could rival Ephesus in this respect.

What made the city particularly famous was its immense temple, dedicated to Diana. This was the biggest shrine, but not the only one, for Ephesus was also a centre for the worship of Emperor Augustus, as well as being a place where congregated all who were interested in spiritism and magic.

In this city there was also an assembly of Christian believers. How did they come to be there? Some of them had been converted in A.D. 30 on the Day of Pentecost, as is recorded for us in Acts 2:9. These would have been Jews. Others had been converted in A.D. 52, during the events described in Acts 18:18-21: 'So Paul still remained a good while [at Corinth]. Then he took leave of the brethren and sailed for Syria, and Priscilla and Aquila were with him. He had his hair cut off at Cenchrea, for he had taken a vow. And he came to Ephesus, and left them there; but he himself entered the synagogue and reasoned with the Jews. When they asked him to stay a longer time with them, he did not consent, but took leave of them, saying, "I must by all means keep this coming feast in Jerusalem; but I will return again to you, God willing."'

Paul was as good as his word, and was at Ephesus again before the year was out, remaining until A.D. 56, three years later. What happened then is recounted in Acts 19: 'God worked unusual miracles by the hands of Paul... Also, many of those who had practised magic brought their books together and burned them in the sight of all. And they counted up the value of them, and it totalled fifty thousand pieces of silver. So the word of the Lord grew mightily and prevailed' (Acts 19:11,19-20).

The apostle's fruitful ministry at Ephesus was cut short by a riot. The message of the ageing preacher proved so powerful that countless numbers of men and women turned from idolatry to faith in Christ. The city's silversmiths, whose livelihood depended on the sale of their miniature replicas of Diana's shrine, feared that they were going to be ruined. It was their pressure which led to a city-wide disturbance, making it impossible for Paul to remain. But the departure of the apostle did not mean the end of the church in Ephesus. Paul kept in contact with it, and once, in A.D. 55 or 56, was able to spend time with its elders, giving to them the message preserved for us in Acts 20:17-38. This is the local church to which he wrote in A.D. 62.

But this does not mean that this letter is for Ephesian eyes only. It is for Christians everywhere. Paul declares that he is writing 'to the saints who are in Ephesus, and faithful in Christ Jesus'. From the very earliest times this letter has been known as the Epistle to the Ephesians. But it is equally true that from A.D. 62 onwards, copies of this letter circulated widely without the words 'in Ephesus' in the opening sentences. It was understood that Paul's probable intention was that his letter, written to a specific church, should also be a circular letter to other churches. What was read at Ephesus was to be read elsewhere. This is why the letter does not single out any individuals for a particular greeting, as is normal in Paul's letters. The only person mentioned by name is Tychicus. We are told that it was he who carried it to Ephesus, and we may safely assume that he took it to other churches too, dropping the words 'in Ephesus', and substituting the name of the local church to which he was reading it. The letter has a general character, and does not address any special situation in any particular church.

Now, of course, letters addressed to particular churches are of great interest to us. The Holy Spirit has preserved a number of these letters for us, such as the epistles to the Philippians and to the Colossians which we have already mentioned. But when a letter is obviously intended to be not only for a specific church, but for all churches, then it attracts our special attention.

3. Because of the spirit in which it comes

Having told us who is writing, and to whom, Paul adds: **'Grace to you and peace from God our Father and the Lord Jesus Christ.'**

Two thousand years ago, when two Greeks met in the street, or elsewhere, they would greet each other by saying *'Chairein'*. The first word of greeting which Paul uses here is a similar word, but it is not identical. It is *'charis'*, translated in our English versions by the word 'grace'. The common greeting among Jews was, and still is, *'Shalom'*. This means 'peace', 'health' or 'wholesomeness'. Paul, then, takes up a Christianized form of the Greek greeting, and the normal Jewish greeting, and uses them in the greeting which immediately follows his opening sentence. But why?

We may breathe a sigh of relief. This letter comes to us with friendly greetings. That is the spirit of the letter. It wishes me grace, it wishes me health, it intends to do me good. But verse 2 shows to us that these greetings do not come to us in Paul's name. They come 'from God our Father and the Lord Jesus Christ'. The letter is a means of grace. By it, our God and Saviour intends to bring us spiritual health.

If Paul were to come and speak to any of us today, we would certainly feel very intimidated, or even petrified. Whatever would he say to us? He was not a man to mince his words, and he could see right through people. For that reason alone we would be in awe of him, especially when we remembered that the Lord Jesus Christ had personally commissioned him to be the apostle to the Gentiles.

But as Paul writes this letter to us, he tells us that he does not want us to feel like that. We are not to feel intimidated at all. His letter comes to us as a friend. Yes, it comes to us from God. Yes, it comes to us from the Lord Jesus Christ. Equally certainly, it comes to us through an illustrious human penman. But it comes to us as a means of grace and spiritual health. We do not need to be on our guard. We have no reason to be cautious or suspicious. No one need be on edge, or afraid, when reading this letter. We are to open our heart to it and to welcome what it teaches. We are to embrace it as the friend that it is.

4. Because of what it is about

There is a further reason for studying the letter to the Ephesians. It is because of what it is about. This is mentioned in verse 3, where Paul refers to **'every spiritual blessing in the heavenly places in Christ'**. This letter is about the enormous privileges which we, as Christians, enjoy. It is therefore also about the responsibilities which we have to fulfil. This is why the first three chapters of the book are doctrinal, while the remaining three are practical.

There are such things as earthly blessings, which all people enjoy to some degree; and there are such things as spiritual blessings, which only some people enjoy. Earthly blessings are the blessings which God gives to men and women simply because they live on this earth. The sun rises on both the evil and the good. The rain falls on both the just and unjust. All who live owe their life to God alone. It is he who gives us the measure of health and strength we have. He it is who gives us our clothes and possessions, employment and leisure, family life and fun, our interests and abilities, and all that we enjoy through the senses.

We do not all have these blessings in equal amounts, but all those we do have come from the same source, which is God himself. This is something we should constantly remember, and the importance of this fact should never be belittled. But these blessings are for this life only. When we finish this life, we leave them behind. We have them while we are in this world, and because we are in this world. God gives them to men and women during their mortal life, whether they have any regard for him or not.

Unconverted people think only of these earthly blessings and, generally, do not care to remember from where they come. Their affections are set upon these things. Their thoughts are taken up with money, health, friends, family, travel and ambition. These are the things that matter to them. In most cases, they consider wealth to be of particular importance, because it makes other earthly blessings easier to acquire.

The Epistle to the Ephesians is not about such things. It is about heavenly blessings. It is about spiritual blessings. There are some people who, besides living in this world, belong to another world. At the moment they live in two worlds, but belong more to the other world than to this one. They see that this world is a passing world. The other world, to which they belong, is an eternal world. It is invisible, but this fact does not make it unreal.

These people are in fellowship with God. They are aware of him, they know him, and they love him. They have come to know him through the Lord Jesus Christ, who is a reality to them. Their life is lived in a different dimension which is distinct from, but not distant from, the dimension in which all men live. This dimension is the world of the invisible, of Christ, of the holy angels. They think about these things, as well as about the spiritual wickedness that there is in high places, against which they must go to war.

These people enjoy the blessings of this present world as much as anybody else. They walk, run and swim like others, listen to music, appreciate nature, and are glad to be alive. They enjoy this world, but enjoy the blessings of the spiritual world more. They know that they will never experience all that this world has to offer. But they do enjoy everything that the spiritual world contains. As they develop spiritually, their pleasure becomes ever fuller and more complete.

What those blessings are, how we come by them, what responsibilities they lay upon us in this life, and how being a member of the other world affects our behaviour here and now — this is the theme of the Epistle to the Ephesians. If we want to know more, this is the letter to study. Once we are convinced of this, we will spare no effort to master its teachings completely.

Do these opening verses tell us very much about these spiritual blessings?

Ephesians, then, is about spiritual blessings. But do these opening verses tell us very much about them? Yes, they do. They lay a foundation on which it is essential to build if we are to really understand the rest of the letter.

1. They tell us from whom they come

In verse 3, Paul cries out: **'Blessed be the God and Father of our Lord Jesus Christ, who has blessed us with every spiritual blessing in the heavenly places in Christ.'**
The blessings of the heavenly world do not belong to anyone naturally. No one is born with them. Nor does anyone earn them, for they are always something given. One person cannot give them to another, not even parents to children, or husbands to wives, or vice-versa.

All who enjoy these blessings remember a time when they did not have them. They can also remember a time when they entered the spiritual dimension and came to possess them. All who have received them can, and do, join with Paul in his doxology. It is from God that these blessings come — not from God the unknown, but from the God and Father of our Lord Jesus Christ.

All the blessings of the heavenly world are given by him. No one can enjoy its blessings without him. But when he gives somebody the blessings of that world, he gives him *all* the blessings that that world contains. Believers are boundlessly rich, even when poor in this world's goods. They have received all the riches that heaven contains, freely given to them by a boundless Giver.

2. They tell us by whom they come

Let us look carefully at Paul's language in this paragraph. In verse 3 he says exultingly, 'Blessed be the God and Father of our Lord Jesus Christ, who has blessed us with every spiritual blessing in the heavenly places *in Christ.*' In verse 4 he continues: **'... just as he chose us *in him'*.** In verse 5 he talks of God **'having predestined us to adoption as sons by *Jesus Christ'*,** while in verse 6 he teaches that God **'has made us accepted *in the Beloved'*.**

God's method is this: all that heaven contains is in the hands of his eternal Son, our Lord Jesus Christ. It follows that when someone receives Christ, he receives all that heaven contains. He is blessed with every spiritual blessing in heavenly places *in Christ*.

The late Dr Ernest Kevan was a great theologian. This was why he was able to explain great truths to small children. I am told that on one occasion he spoke to boys and girls with a set of large coloured wooden bricks beside him. The bricks were of various sizes and fitted into each other, so that the whole set could be carried inside the largest brick. The smallest brick, I believe, was called 'perseverance'. He explained to the children what this meant. This was then fitted into a larger brick called 'sanctification'. In simple terms he showed the children that there is no perseverance without sanctification. We continue to the end because God makes us holy. 'Sanctification' was then put inside 'adoption'. There would be no holiness if we were not the adopted children of God. 'Adoption' was then fitted into 'justification'. How can anyone be a child of God without first being right with God?

At this stage Dr Kevan had only one brick left beside him. It was the largest of all, and on it was written 'The Lord Jesus Christ'. He went over what he had already taught, showing how each blessing was in another. Coming to his conclusion, he said, 'And so you see...' They were the last words of his address. A small boy, his hand raised, called out, 'Please sir, it's all in Christ.' The man of God said no more, and closed the service with a hymn.

Every spiritual blessing that exists is in Christ. We receive them on no other condition than being in Christ. Once someone has received the Lord Jesus Christ, there is nothing more for him to receive. The greater blessing includes all the lesser ones. It may be that the believer does not yet fully appreciate how very rich he is, and does not yet have full enjoyment of all these blessings. But this in no way alters the fact that he has received them.

All that was necessary to procure these blessings was done by Christ, by his perfect life and his shocking death. And what he has procured does not come into our hands by any other way but by him. This is why, of course, there is no other way of salvation. All spiritual blessings are in Christ, so if someone is not in Christ, he has no spiritual blessings at all. This is true, however moral and religious he may be. Paul's teaching is a million miles away from much modern teaching which promises eternal life to the heathen, and to others, on the basis of 'a good life', and whether they have heard of Christ or not.

3. They tell us why they come to us and not to all men and women

We now know from whom spiritual blessings come, and by whom. But why do they come to us and not to all men and women? How is it that *we* are the ones who are justified, adopted, sanctified and persevering? Why me? Every believer has asked this question at some time or other. Many of us have family members and friends who are not yet in Christ. We are no better than they are. We are certainly not more intelligent or discerning. They have qualities in their characters which shame us. How is it, then, that we have come to possess every spiritual blessing in Christ, while countless others live and die without ever knowing such a glorious privilege?

Paul gives a plain answer to our question. **'[God] chose us in him before the foundation of the world,'** he writes, **'... having predestined us to adoption as sons by Jesus Christ to himself, according to the good pleasure of his will'** (1:4-5). The reason why some enter into the boundless riches of heaven in the Lord Jesus Christ lies in God, and not in us.

Let us pause, to listen to some wonderful words from John Calvin's commentary on Ephesians: 'The foundation and first cause, both of our calling and of all the benefits which we receive from God, is here declared to be his eternal election. If the reason is asked why God has called us to enjoy the gospel, why he daily bestows upon us so many blessings, why he opens to us the gate of heaven — the answer will be constantly found in this principle, that he hath *chosen us before the foundation of the world*. The very time when the election took place proves it to be free; for what could we have deserved, or what merit did we possess, before the world was made?'

What a marvellous truth! God's plan of salvation is no last-minute affair. In all its details, it was decided before the foundation of the world. By all means let us say that we do not understand this. Let some be honest enough to say that they do not like it. But let no one say that he does not believe it, lest he be found to contradict the great apostle to the Gentiles and, worse, the Lord himself who inspired his apostle to teach this truth.

Let every believer think it through. Before Adam fell; before the
world was made; even before an angel ever prostrated himself
before Jehovah's throne; when there was nothing but God in the
eternal concert of his three majestic Persons — then the thoughts of
God were upon you! These thoughts were loving thoughts, deciding
that every spiritual blessing in heavenly places should be yours, in
Christ. Such thoughts have been in God's mind for as long as he has
been God!

4. They tell us for what purpose these blessings are given

These opening verses tell us from whom spiritual blessings come,
by whom, and why they come to some and not others. But that is not
all. They also reveal for what purpose these blessings are given.

On this point, Paul has two things to say. The first is in verse 6.
Here he teaches us that God has given us these blessings '**... to the
praise of the glory of his grace, by which he has made us
accepted in the Beloved'**.

If you are a Christian today, it is because of God's undeserved
kindness, or grace. He chose you, and the Good Shepherd gave his
life for you, long before you ever knew about him. Then he found
you, lost sheep that you were. He did it all. It is all of grace —
glorious grace, God's grace. His intention in saving us is that there
should be an innumerable company of people who, throughout
eternity, would praise the glory of his grace. How awful it would be
if our eternal song of praise was only about his justice or his power!
Thanks be to God, it will not be like that. Here on earth we have
already started to acclaim and to glorify God's grace. There we shall
do it perfectly, ceaselessly and endlessly!

Paul's other point is in verse 4. God has saved as he has '**... that
we should be holy and without blame before him'**. He desires,
even in this life, that there should be people who are different from
all the rest, people who are evidently living in two worlds, and not
just this one. Positively, he desires that their characters should be
more and more similar to that of the one who has poured out such
blessings on them. They are to be holy. This is to be their ambition,
and they are to give themselves to pursuing it. Negatively, they are
to be without blame. They are to make a similar effort to live
unblemished lives. They are to put away everything doubtful,
everything which God's searching and ever-present eye does not

applaud. He has not saved them so that they can remain as they were, but for them to be like him in this world, and eternally with him in the next.

The two points we have just mentioned crystallize the outline of the rest of the book. God's grace is the dominant theme of the first three chapters. Practical holiness is the subject of the last three. Our study of the first six verses has helpfully prepared us for what is going to follow.

2.
Every spiritual blessing!

Please read Ephesians 1:3-14

Keeping everything we have learned in mind, we come to explore more fully this subject of spiritual blessings. We do this by looking closely at Ephesians 1:3-14. Our passage thus overlaps our previous study but that does not matter, for we have so much to discover. There are three types of spiritual blessings which believers enjoy. If we search the whole of the paragraph before us, it will become plain what they are.

Blessings for the present

1. Adoption

There are certain privileges which Christians enjoy now. If you are a Christian, you are enjoying them at this moment, as you sit and read this book. The first one which Paul mentions here is adoption. In verse 5, he says that God has blessed us, **'having predestined us to adoption as sons by Jesus Christ to himself, according to the good pleasure of his will'**. The relationship which we have to the great God is that of children to their Father! We are his sons. This glorious prerogative is not enjoyed by anyone at all, except Christian believers. The Bible does not teach anywhere the universal fatherhood of God and the universal brotherhood of men, but it does say that 'As many as received him [Christ], to them he gave the right to become children of God, even to those who believe in his name' (John 1:12).

The sonship of which we are speaking is not natural, but adoptive. And it is the highest privilege which the gospel gives us. It is a wonderful thing to know that the Judge has declared us 'not guilty'. That is the truth of justification, and no other blessing could be ours if we were not right with God. Justification is the foundation blessing of the Christian life. But this does not mean that it is the highest. What if the judge should take the criminal home and adopt him into his family, put his name upon him, give to him all the pleasure and benefits of his own home, and be a father to him? This is what God has done to us in Christ.

What is a Christian? A Christian is someone who has God as his or her Father. That is the simplest definition, and it is the best. Once this is clear, so much else becomes clear. Why should Christians behave differently? Because they are to take on the family likeness (Matt. 5:48). How are they to pray? As children speak to their father (Matt. 6:9). Why are they not to worry about the supply of their needs? Because their heavenly Father cares about them (Matt. 6:31-32). This wonderful strand of teaching, hardly known in Old Testament days, comes into its own in the gospel, which is why Paul reminds us of it here.

But to fully appreciate and value what Paul is saying, we must put certain ideas out of our minds. In the early world, adoption was not as it often is today. Babies were not adopted, but adults. If a rich person had no natural heir to whom he could leave his riches, he would look round for someone outside his family who would be worthy of inheriting his wealth. He would then adopt him. Absolutely everything he had was now going to go into good hands. It was this practice which Paul had in mind when he spoke of adoption.

Once this is understood, the Bible's teaching on this point can only be seen as startling. God does not adopt people of proven worth. He does not give his treasures to people who are outstanding. Adoption is not a reward for holy living. God adopts wrongdoers. He enriches failures. He makes rebels his heirs. What grace — grace that is greater than all our sin!

2. *Acceptance*

Where there is adoption there is inevitably acceptance. This is spoken about in verse 6, where Paul states that God **'has made us accepted in the Beloved'**.

To understand what this means we need only to think of the parable of the prodigal son. Far from home, destitute and feeding the pigs, the prodigal decided to return home. He would not ask to be received back into the family, but would ask his father to take him on as a hired servant. But this was not to be. 'When he was still a great way off, his father saw him and had compassion, and ran and fell on his neck and kissed him' (Luke 15:20). Moments later the son's shame was covered by his father's best robe. A ring on his hand testified to all that he had been fully reinstated as a son. Shoes on his feet witnessed that he was a free man, and not in any sense a slave. His repentance and return were greeted with joy and celebration.

Now why did the father not treat the prodigal as a servant? Why did he give him a festive welcome? It was because he was his son. This being so, how could his acceptance be anything other than unconditional and complete?

This is how our heavenly Father treats us. We end each day with our lives stained by sin. Our thoughts have not been totally pure. Our lips have spoken unwise, and often unkind, words. We have not done what we should have done, and we most certainly have done what we should not have done. But does this mean that God has turned his back on us? As we seek his face in repentant prayer, we discover that he welcomes us without any reserve. We have been in the far country, but he has been waiting for us. When we turn to him, he runs to meet us, even when we are still a great way off. He throws his arms around us and treats us as dear children. He never hesitates. We approach him with tears, but find that his home is a house of joy.

How is it that the just and holy God can give us such a reception? It is because his eternal Son has never disappointed him in any way, and he sees us as being in him. He accepts us for Christ's sake. In our unholiest moments, in the depths of our backsliding, even then the righteousness of Christ is reckoned to our account, and the Father sees us as having no faults. There is no cloud between us and our God, not ever. There is no obstacle to our communion with him. We have never done anything but fail. There is not an ounce of worthiness in any of us. But God himself has made us accepted in the Beloved. It is nothing to do with us, and everything to do with him. We are back to the theme of grace. Our souls are stained crimson by the number of our crimes. But it is all washed away. In God's eyes we are whiter than snow. And all because of what he has done for us in our Lord Jesus Christ. What blessings we enjoy right now!

Blessings from the past

Yes, it is sinners that God adopts and accepts. But how can he do this, seeing that he is just and holy? How can the Pure One embrace the impure? He knows how defiled we are, for nothing anywhere is hidden from him. He knows the depths of our sins in all their details. On what basis can he receive us so unreservedly? It is because of two blessings to do with the past.

1. Redemption

One of these is redemption. **'In [Christ] we have redemption through his blood,'** says the apostle in verse 7. This word means to 'buy back' or to 'repurchase'. When people buy back articles they have left with the pawnbroker, they 'redeem' them. In the Old Testament, if a man raised money by selling his land, he had a God-given right to 'redeem' it, or buy it back, when he had sufficient funds to do so. Men and women who sold themselves into slavery could do the same, or they could be redeemed by someone else handing over the required sum of money. Freedom came through the paying of a price!

Our Lord Jesus Christ came to redeem. When she had seen the infant Messiah, Anna 'spoke of him to all those who looked for redemption in Jerusalem' (Luke 2:38). The Saviour himself declared that he had 'not come to be served, but to serve, and to give his life a ransom for many' (Mark 10:45). He drew attention to the same concept when, at the Last Supper, he spoke of his blood being 'shed for many for the remission of sins' (Matt. 26:28).

Paul's language in his epistles is equally clear. To the Galatians, he writes, 'Christ has redeemed us from the curse of the law, having become a curse for us' (Gal. 3:13). He reminds the Romans that we are 'justified freely by his grace through the redemption that is in Christ Jesus' (Rom. 3:24). We have been redeemed. We have been bought back. The price has been paid. Christ paid that price when he shed his blood on the cross. It is the price we should have paid ourselves, but he has paid it instead.

2. Forgiveness

This being so, we have forgiveness. In Paul's mind, 'redemption' and 'forgiveness' cannot be separated. This is why he writes as he does in verse 7. Speaking of our Lord Jesus Christ, he says, **'In him we have redemption through his blood, the forgiveness of sins, according to the riches of his grace.'**

There is a price to be paid for breaking the law of God. It is infinite punishment. We have broken that law, and justice demands that we pay the price. But the Saviour has come and done what we could never do. The infinite God-man has paid the infinite price. He has completely paid it. There is nothing left for us to pay. We have no debt. We are free. We are forgiven.

Jesus spoke of forgiveness in terms of paying a debt. He taught us to pray to our Father: 'And forgive us our debts, as we forgive our debtors' (Matt. 6:12). The same emphasis comes across in the parable of the unforgiving servant in Matthew 18:21-35. In this story, a king does not insist that one of his servants should pay back an immense sum of money that he owes him. He lets him off. In other words, he forgives him. But this servant will not let off someone who owes him a much smaller debt. He is unforgiving and is ultimately punished by the king for it. 'So my heavenly Father also will do to you if each of you, from his heart, does not forgive his brother his trespasses' (Matt. 18:35).

Our own debt to God cannot be measured, and we cannot pay it. But God does not cancel our debt by a wave of the hand. Justice demands that the debt be paid. And it has been! God's abounding love paid it, when the Saviour died in our place. Justice will not demand that the same debt be paid twice. I am forgiven! What God has done in the past guarantees the blessings we enjoy in the present. Adopted, accepted, there is nothing to pay!

> Nothing to pay! Ah, nothing to pay!
> Never a word of excuse to say!
> Year after year thou hast filled the score,
> Owing thy Lord still more and more.
> Hear the voice of Jesus say,
> 'Verily thou hast nothing to pay!
> Ruined, lost art thou, and yet
> I forgave thee all that debt!'

Nothing to pay! The debt is so great;
What will you do with the awful weight?
How shall the way of escape be made?
Nothing to pay! Yet it must be paid!
Hear the voice of Jesus say,
'Verily thou hast nothing to pay!
All has been put to my account,
I have paid the full amount.'

Nothing to pay! Yes, nothing to pay!
Jesus has cleared all the debt away,
Blotted it out with his bleeding hand!
Free and forgiven, and loved, you stand.
Hear the voice of Jesus say,
'Verily thou hast nothing to pay!
Paid is the debt and the debtor free!
Now I ask thee, lovest thou me?'

(Frances Ridley Havergal, 1836-79).

Blessings for the future

There is no cloud between me and my God. I am his adopted son —
accepted, welcomed and loved. What does the future hold for me?

The answer to this question is no secret. This is made clear in
verses 8-10. Verse 8 tells us that God has lavished the riches of his
grace upon us. An evidence of this is that we have been given
wisdom and understanding. As others think about the future, they
are left wondering and guessing. But we are not!

God has made known to us the mystery of his will (1:9). He has
revealed it to apostles, like Paul, and they have passed it on to us. We
are in on the secret. God has plans which depend upon no one but
himself. The reasons for them lie in him alone. And yet it is his will
that we should know what he has in store.

God controls history, and when his time is ripe he will bring to
pass what he has always intended to do (1:10). And what is that? The
time is coming when all things shall be under the rule of Christ. This
present rebellious universe will not always remain in defiance. Soon
there will not be any sort of authority in it anywhere, except that of
the Lord Jesus Christ. All delegated authority will be gone and he

will rule directly. All who have shown dissatisfaction with him will acknowledge him as Lord. The universe, thrown into disorientation through man's sin, will be brought back to its original orderliness and unity as everything, everywhere, submits to Christ. This does not mean that everyone is, at last, going to be saved. But it does mean that those who have mocked him will see him elevated. No other name will be honoured, 'that at the name of Jesus every knee should bow, of those in heaven, and of those on earth, and of those under the earth, and that every tongue should confess that Jesus Christ is Lord, to the glory of God the Father' (Phil. 2:10-11). Unconverted men and women do not even think about such a climactic ending to history. But it is no secret to us.

1. Our inheritance

It is at that time we shall enter into our inheritance (1:11). As adopted children, the inheritance is ours now, but we shall enjoy full possession of it then. The Father chose us for this. He himself has decided our destination. We have been predestined.

And there is no chance that we shall fail to arrive in the promised glory. What could stop us? Without being responsible for its sin, God personally controls what happens in his universe. He has foreordained whatever comes to pass. He governs all his creatures and all their actions. **'[He] works all things according to the counsel of his will'** (1:11). Everything, everywhere, is bringing to pass the eternal purpose of God. And within that purpose he has planned that his redeemed and adopted people should safely enter into their inheritance, **'that we who first trusted in Christ should be to the praise of his glory'** (1:12).

Oh, what riches await us! How the Bible excites us as it speaks about the future! Sooner than we dare believe, we shall be with Christ. Our bodies will be resurrected to be like his glorious body. Our characters will be perfectly holy, and therefore perfectly happy. Sin will have gone and, therefore, the curse. We shall be where there are no more tears. Death will be no more, nor will there be any form of sorrow or pain. We shall bask in the light of the Lamb of God, enjoying perfect fellowship with him, with his elect people and with the holy angels. Nothing will spoil this — ever. Everything will be new. The new creation will be a world of divine beauty and love. And God will be all in all.

2. We are sealed

Seeing that countless millions are going to be welcomed into the final glory, is it possible that God might overlook me? Not at all! None of God's people will be forgotten. The apostle puts to flight our fears by telling us in verses 13-14 that the entry of each believer is *guaranteed.*

This is because something wonderful happens to each Christian at the moment he believes. God puts a mark on him. **'You were sealed,'** says Paul. What is he telling us? He is referring to a practice which both he and the Ephesians understood very well. Cargo belonging to several merchants would travel on the same ship. Who was to know which boxes belonged to which merchant? Every merchant had his own distinctive sign or 'seal'. Everything that belonged to him carried that mark. Whatever did not carry that mark obviously belonged to somebody else.

All believers have been sealed. Verse 13 says so, and Paul will make the point again in 4:30. Having believed, they were sealed with the promised Holy Spirit. This sealing is not something the Holy Spirit does. The seal *is* the Holy Spirit. All who have trusted in Christ through hearing the word of truth, the gospel of salvation, have received the Holy Spirit. The fact that he is in their life is proof that they belong to the Master. They will be unloaded at the right port and will go to the right destination.

To underline this point, Paul uses a different illustration in verse 14. Here he says that the Holy Spirit **'is the guarantee of our inheritance'**. The Greek word translated 'guarantee' is also taken from the world of commerce. If a trader wishes to buy something, but does not have all the money required, he leaves a deposit with whoever is selling what he wants. This deposit is a pledge to buy the goods and a promise to return with the full amount necessary. It is a down payment guaranteeing that there will be more to follow.

This is exactly the Holy Spirit's role. He is given to us at the moment of believing. We receive him on the simple condition of being in Christ. And why is he given? It is to show us that all we have been promised will certainly be ours. He **'is the guarantee of our inheritance until the redemption of the purchased possession'** (1:14). In fact, we ourselves are the possession that God has purchased. The Lord will return for us and take us home. The down payment which has been given declares to all that this is a fact. Nobody who bears the divine mark will be overlooked. But we should remember that the opposite is also true. Those who do not bear that mark will not be glorified, for 'If anyone does not have the Spirit of Christ, he is not his' (Rom. 8:9).

How important it is to know that we have received the Holy Spirit! To know this is to know we have become true Christians. Those who have not received the Holy Spirit are not even Christians at all. Those who have not been sealed have no mark of ownership upon them. It is a grave mistake to assume that they are some sort of defective or inferior believer. The fact is that they do not belong to the Master but to Satan.

To ask someone, 'Have you been sealed with the Holy Spirit?' is the same as asking him if he is a believer. It is asking him whether he has the mark of ownership which is the guarantee of his final entry into the future inheritance.

Wherever the Holy Spirit enters a life, three things happen to the person concerned: he comes to believe the truth about our Lord Jesus Christ — about who he is and what he has done; he comes to love God's demands as found in his Word, and to sincerely attempt to implement them; he comes to love other believers more than any other group of people on earth, and lives to forward their welfare. The proof of the Spirit's presence is thus doctrinal, moral and social. He brings men and women to believe and to behave differently. The gift of tongues does not prove the Spirit to be present, because plenty of people who follow other gods exercise that gift. Nor are elated feelings a sign, because you can get similar emotions from certain drugs. The Holy Spirit brings about what no one can counterfeit. He brings about a spiritual change for which God gets the glory (1:14).

Isn't it wonderful to be a Christian? In this life, now, we know God, have the privilege of being his children, and are unhesitatingly accepted by him. Our consciences are at peace because the Saviour has paid the price we should have paid, and God has forgiven us our every sin. We do not fear the future — not the grave, not the resurrection, and not the judgement — because we know what the ultimate outcome will be. In due time, everything will be centred on Christ and subject to him. Then we shall enter into our inheritance. The guarantee of this has already been given to us.

Who is richer than we are? Only the Giver, who has granted us all this by pure grace. Blessed be the God and Father of our Lord Jesus Christ, who has blessed us with every spiritual blessing in the heavenly places in Christ!

3.
Three questions — and ten objections

Once more, please read Ephesians 1:3-14

Those who have listened to Paul's teaching on spiritual blessings usually have a number of questions in their minds. There are three which are particularly common, and Ephesians 1:3-14 gives an answer to each one. We shall look at these first.

Paul's answers do not always meet with the approval of those who hear them. They raise objections, and we shall consider the ten which are most frequently voiced. Not everyone will agree that this should be done in a commentary such as this. But if we have reservations about what Paul says in his first chapter, how shall we derive any real profit from the rest?

Three questions

1. How do we enter into these spiritual blessings?

It is on the simple condition of being 'in Christ'. This is a point Paul stresses throughout our paragraph. '[God] has blessed us with every spiritual blessing in the heavenly places *in Christ* ... he chose us *in him* ... having predestined us to adoption as sons *by Jesus Christ* to himself ... he has made us accepted *in the Beloved. In him* we have redemption ... that he might gather together in one all things *in Christ* ... *in him* ... *in whom* also we have obtained an inheritance' (1:3,4,5,6,7,10,11, italics mine). It is too obvious to miss. Like the small boy who saw Dr Kevan's bricks, we should cry out, 'Please sir, it's all in Christ!'

2. How is Christ received?

This is made clear in verses 12 and 13. God has done what he has done, says Paul, **'that we who first trusted in Christ should be to the praise of his glory'**. There Paul probably has his own experience in mind. But the Ephesians had come to faith in Christ in just the same way. So he continues, **'In him you also trusted, after you heard the word of truth, the gospel of your salvation; in whom also, having believed, you were sealed with the Holy Spirit of promise.'**

Heaven's riches become ours when we trust in Christ. We hear the truth about him. We believe it to be true. And then we commit ourselves to what we have come to know and believe. We depend upon it. We put our whole weight upon it — not just on a series of truths, but on the person proclaimed in those truths.

This is precisely what had happened to the Ephesians. They had heard the word of truth, the gospel which announced salvation. They knew how holy God was, and how awful it was to be unlike him. They knew that they deserved infinite punishment for their sins. They knew that only God's eternal Son, the Lord Jesus Christ, had ever lived sinlessly. They knew that when he died it could not have been for his own sins, and it was therefore for the sins of others. They knew that there was no hope for sinners except in Christ. They knew that they had to repent and to turn again to the God whom they had offended. All this they knew. They believed it to be true. And they acted upon it. They did turn to God, believing that he would accept them for the sake of Christ. They trusted the Saviour. And so it was that they came to be 'in Christ' and to have every spiritual blessing in him.

3. Why us, and not others?

Many people do not know the gospel for they have never heard it. That was not true of Paul, nor of the Ephesian believers, nor of us. Others have heard the gospel, but do not believe it to be true. Yet others have heard the gospel and believe it to be true, but stop there. They never actually come to depend on the Lord Jesus Christ. They do not trust him. This raises certain questions in every believer's mind : 'Why am I not like those people? What makes me different? Why have I come to be saved, when they have not?'

Paul's inspired answer leaps from the page in front of us. If we have any spiritual blessings at all, it is because God gave them to us, and he is the one who must be praised (1:3). But why, oh why, did he give them to *us*? It is because **'He chose us [in Christ] before the foundation of the world ... having predestined us ... according to the good pleasure of his will'** (1:4-5). The reason for his choice, then, is found in him and not in us.

Were we more deserving than others? No, because he did what he did **'to the praise of the glory of his grace'** (1:6). The source of God's election is to be found in his loving-kindness, and in that alone. He deals with us **'according to the riches of his grace which he made to abound towards us'** (1:7-8). He does it **'according to his good pleasure which he purposed in himself'** (1:9). There is no escaping what God's Word is teaching here. The reason that people are saved is that they are **'predestined according to the purpose of him who works all things according to the counsel of his will'** (1:11).

All who are saved are saved by God's grace. Nothing has moved him to save us except his own heart. He desired to do it out of his own good pleasure. It is undeserved love streaming from the very essence of God that has brought us out of our condition of sin and misery into the everlasting comfort of salvation. How we should glorify God for his grace!

This, too, is a theme Paul touches on here. God has predestined us to be to the praise of the glory of his grace (1:5-6). He has saved us that we **'should be to the praise of his glory'** (1:12,14). In heaven we shall give him the praise that he deserves. But the epistle will teach us that we are to glorify him for his grace in the here and now, and that we are to do it with both our lips and our lives.

Before we leave our three questions and answers, let us bring home one more important truth. No one enters into spiritual blessings without divine election. We must therefore never play down what the Bible teaches about God's sovereign grace. We must never blur the edges, or blunt the sharpness of anything that God has revealed. We must never alter what the Lord has spoken in the hope of making it easier for man to accept. Grace is the theme of heaven and it should be our theme on earth. We should declare what the Bible teaches both boldly and warmly. He loved us because he loved us. We love him because he first loved us. We did not choose him, but he chose us.

This said, we must remember that no elect person enters into any spiritual blessing whatever without trusting in Christ. And nobody trusts in Christ without hearing the word of truth, the gospel of salvation. Just as surely as God has decreed who will be saved, so has he decreed by what means men and women will be brought to salvation. It is through the proclamation of the truth. It is through the spreading of the gospel. There is, then, no contradiction between the doctrines of grace and the practice of biblical evangelism. Both are found together and it is impossible to separate them. We are as enthusiastic about one as we are about the other. Evangelism would be a perpetual failure if election were not true. But it is thrilling to those who believe what God says about his eternal decrees. Each conversion is then seen for what it is — the accomplishment in time and space of an eternal plan. We see unfolding before our eyes what God planned in eternity. We have no idea who the elect are. We find out, as we see one and another coming to faith in the Lord Jesus Christ.

Ten objections

We must now deal with some common objections to the doctrine of election. The following paragraphs will not interest many of you who read this book. Ephesians 1:1-14 conquered your hearts long ago and you are at peace with its teachings. You experience no stress or tension when you hear about predestination and election. But you might care to remember that it was not always like that. When many of you heard these truths for the first time, they kept you awake at night. Others of you were filled with rebellion, so that you almost felt like giving up the Christian faith. Others of you accepted these truths, but for a while the effect on your life was to make you very brittle, and antagonistic to other Christians.

Other readers are still finding Paul's teaching on election rather strange and more than difficult to believe. You sincerely doubt whether the interpretation of Ephesians 1:3-14 you have just read is a correct understanding of the Word of God. The questions and answers which follow are not intended to prove that I am right and you are wrong. Their purpose is simply to help you come to settled conclusions in your own thinking through a fuller consideration of what the Scriptures teach.

1. God's election is based on his foreknowledge

This view believes that God, being all-knowing, looked down history and saw beforehand who would believe. He then chose those people to be his children. To back up this conviction, this view appeals to Romans 8:29: 'For whom he foreknew, he also predestined to be conformed to the image of his Son, that he might be the first-born among many brethren.' It also appeals to 1 Peter 1:2: 'elect according to the foreknowledge of God the Father'.

In English dictionaries the word 'foreknow' means 'to know in advance'. In the Bible, its meaning is much fuller. In Acts 2:23 Peter, preaching on the Day of Pentecost, says that Jesus was delivered to the cross 'by the carefully planned intention and foreknowledge of God'. To him, foreknowledge clearly meant predetermination.

Of equal interest is the Bible's use of the word 'know'. It often means 'to love intimately' and is the normal word used to describe the deep love expressed in the marriage bond. So when God says to Israel, 'You only have I known of all the families of the earth' (Amos 3:2), he is talking of his deep love for the nation which had led him to choose it as his own. The Good Shepherd uses the verb in exactly the same sense when he says, 'I know my sheep' (John 10:14).

This is how the verb 'to foreknow' is used in Romans 8:29, which we have quoted above. It is particular people who are foreknown here, and not something done by them. God predestined them to be conformed to the image of his Son, because he had intimately loved them beforehand. In the same way, we can understand 1 Peter 1:2 to mean 'elect because intimately loved beforehand by God'.

The view expressing this objection believes that God elects us because he sees that we are going to believe. It holds that election is caused by believing. But this is not so. The exact opposite is true. Believing is caused by election: 'And as many as had been appointed to eternal life believed' (Acts 13:48).

2. God elects races and nations, not individuals

This is exactly what Paul is *not* saying in Ephesians 1:3-14. Writing to the individual men and women and children who made up Christ's church at Ephesus and elsewhere, he says, 'God has blessed *us* ... he chose *us*, having predestined *us* ... he has made *us* accepted in the Beloved ... *we* have obtained an inheritance, being predestined ... that *we* who first trusted in Christ should be to the praise of his glory' 1:3-6,11-12, italics mine). It is individuals who have trusted Christ who are assured of their election. There is not a race or nation in sight.

The same is true in Romans 9-11, where Paul deals at greater length with the truth of election. Individuals are in mind. Isaac was chosen, but not Ishmael. Jacob was chosen, but not Esau. Individual branches are stripped from the olive tree that individual branches might be grafted in. Election is individual. Before the world was made, God chose me! That is the wonder of it all.

3. But God is not willing that any should perish

You are right! '"As I live", says the Lord God, "I have no pleasure in the death of the wicked"' (Ezek. 33:11). 'The Lord is ... not willing that any should perish but that all should come to repentance' (2 Peter 3:9).

How do we know that God does not want the wicked to perish? From the Bible! And how do we know that he has chosen certain people to be saved in an eternal decree of election? From the Bible! Let's not use the Bible to contradict the Bible. Let's not say, 'The parts of the Bible I like I will accept, but the parts I don't like I won't accept.' If we were to pick and choose like that, we would be putting our own reason above God's Word. Believing the Book means believing it all. Submitting to Scripture means embracing all that it says. We accept one truth and we accept the other; and both of them we accept gladly, because they are taught in the Word of God. What we do *not* accept is that human minds can plumb this mystery. How can both truths be equally true? It is too deep for us. We are too limited and, besides, our reasoning powers are spoiled by sin. We bow before the mystery, but we cannot explain it.

4. But salvation is offered to 'whoever'!

Once more, you are right. 'For God so loved the world that he gave his only begotten Son, that whoever believes in him should not perish but have everlasting life' (John 3:16). 'For the Scripture says, "Whoever believes on him will not be put to shame." For there is no distinction between Jew and Greek, for the same Lord over all is rich to all who call upon him. For "whoever calls upon the name of the Lord shall be saved"' (Rom. 10:11-13).

All who want to be saved can be saved! God's Word is clear about this. Whoever you are, if you call on the Lord he will save you. This is God's promise and he will not break it. If you are unconverted as you read this, all the blessings of the gospel may be yours, now, if you will but turn from your sin to God, approaching him through the Lord Jesus Christ.

The problem is that men and women, left to themselves, do not want to be saved. The door of salvation is open, but they refuse to walk through it. Why is this? It is because man is a fallen creature. His whole nature is twisted and polluted by sin. He is spiritually dead. He will never move in a Godward direction unless God himself moves him in that way.

John 3:16 is gloriously true. But we should not forget that it is preceded by John 1:12-13: 'But as many as received him, to them he gave the right to become children of God, even to those who believe in his name: who were born, not of blood, nor of the will of the flesh, nor of the will of man, but of God.' Whoever wants to be saved may be so. But no one believes unless his nature is changed. No one's nature is changed, except by God. But why does God change some people's nature, and not others? Ephesians 1:3-14 has given us the answer. It is because he has chosen to.

Romans 10:11-13 is also gloriously true. But before Romans 10 comes Romans 9, where we read, 'For he says to Moses, "I will have mercy on whom I will have mercy, and I will have compassion on whom I will have compassion." So then it is not of him who wills, nor of him who runs, but of God who shows mercy... Therefore he has mercy on whom he wills, and whom he wills he hardens' (Rom. 9:15-16,18).

God's Word most certainly offers salvation to 'whoever'. It also most certainly teaches unconditional election. We must do the same. If we do not, we shall have invented our own religious system. The Bible calls that idolatry.

5. But it isn't fair!

If there was anyone, anywhere, who deserved to be saved, but ended up lost, there would be some strength in this objection. The objection would also stand if the whole human race was composed of people deserving to be saved, with God choosing some and passing the others by.

But that is not the way it is, is it? Every man and woman, every boy and girl on earth is not only a sinner, but a willing sinner. He or she is in deliberate rebellion against God and wants to be the person he or she is. The guilt of all is plain. The wonder is that God saves anybody at all!

The eternal decree of election must be fair, because it is God's decree of election. God, by definition, is fair.

> 'He is the Rock, his work is perfect;
> For all his ways are justice,
> A God of truth and without injustice;
> Righteous and upright is he'
>
> (Deut. 32:4).

Do we believe that, or don't we? If God has done something, then it is fair. If it is unfair, then God has not done it. This remains true whether we can see it or not. We do not see things as God does.

It is monstrous even to think of pointing the finger at God. 'Indeed, O man, who are you to reply against God? Will the thing formed say to him who formed it, "Why have you made me like this?" Does not the potter have power over the clay, from the same lump to make one vessel for honour and another for dishonour? What if God, wanting to show his wrath and to make his power known, endured with much long-suffering the vessels of wrath prepared for destruction, and that he might make known the riches of his glory on the vessels of mercy, which he had prepared beforehand for glory, even us whom he called, not of the Jews only, but also of the Gentiles?' (Rom. 9:20-24).

6. A belief in election kills evangelism

'God's will is always accomplished, isn't it? Seeing he has decided that certain people will be saved, there is no possibility that they will fail to be converted. Whatever we do, or don't do, they will come to faith. So what is the point of evangelism?'

There are some people who talk like that — usually those who are caricaturing the doctrine of election with a view to believing something else. Speaking for myself, I have never heard anyone who loves the doctrine of election speaking in that way — not even once.

The reason that we proclaim the gospel to all is that the Lord Jesus Christ commands us to do so (Matt. 28:18-20). Because we love him, we keep his commandments (John 14:15). It is the love of Christ that constrains us (2 Cor. 5:14). We would go to the work whether anyone was converted through it or not.

As it is, the doctrine of election fills us with optimism. We know that God has not only determined *who* will believe, but *how* they will be brought to faith in Christ. 'Faith comes by hearing, and hearing by the word of God' (Rom. 10:17). Nobody, left to himself, will ever believe. It is the proclamation of God's Word which generates faith in the hearts of those whom God has chosen. How could we ever be discouraged? It is by biblical evangelism that God will bring home his people! Would he send us to any particular place if there were not any elect there? We do not know who they are, and so we sincerely declare the gospel to all. We relate God's promises to 'whoever'. We assure them that God takes no pleasure in the death of the wicked. And we know that God will certainly use the faithful heralding of the gospel to bring about conversions.

The doctrine of election does not kill evangelism. It inspires it. Two thousand years of church history well illustrate this point. Wherever election has been fervently believed there has been an evangelistic spirit. The Reformation was the greatest evangelistic movement since the Acts of the Apostles and the Bible's teaching on election was at its very centre. Most of the great preachers of the eighteenth-century Awakening passionately loved this truth. And countless persevering soul-winners love it still.

We know that the Good Shepherd has died for his sheep. We also know that when those sheep hear his voice, they will follow him. So we sound out the Good Shepherd's word wherever we can! Election stops us from giving up. This was Paul's experience as he evangelized Corinth. There had been a few conversions, but the overall response was one of opposition. 'Now the Lord spoke to Paul in the night by a vision, "Do not be afraid, but speak, and do not keep silent; for I am with you, and no one will attack you to hurt you; for I have many people in this city." And he continued there a year and six months, teaching the word of God among them' (Acts 18:9-11). What kept him going when the response was so unpromising? It was the knowledge that God had a people there. God's decree of election meant that there would be a certain harvest. So he stayed on and preached, and began to see that harvest being reaped.

Election does not kill evangelism. It is the mainspring which drives it. It moves us to take the message to the very worst, even to those who oppose all that we say. In the final analysis, the salvation of men and women does not depend on them, nor on us, but on God; and therefore there is hope.

7. But God loves everybody alike — how can election be true?

God is indeed good to all men and women alike. His sun rises on both the evil and the good. He sends rain on the just and the unjust. But that he loves all men and women alike is not taught anywhere in the Word of God. What does Paul say in Romans 9:10-13? 'But when Rebecca also had conceived by one man, even by our father Isaac (for the children not yet being born, nor having done any good or evil, that the purpose of God according to election might stand, not of works but of him who calls), it was said to her, "The older shall serve the younger." As it is written, "Jacob I have loved, but Esau I have hated."'

Those who have never grasped this will always have problems with the doctrine of election. God's love is a distinguishing love. He is good to all but he does not love all. He gives blessings to some that he does not give to others. And this is true of spiritual blessings.

8. Even if it's true, shouldn't it be kept a secret?

More than one person has said, 'I am a Calvinist on my knees and an Arminian on my feet.' Others tell us to pray as if everything depended on God, but to preach as if it all depended on man. Behind all this is the idea that we should keep our knowledge of election to ourselves and not speak of it to others — and certainly not to unbelievers.

This is absurd. Let us think it out. In communion with God, am I to rejoice in his eternal decrees, and then never to mention to others what has caused my heart to dance? Are we, in our prayer meetings, to take courage from the fact that God has a people whom he will surely save through the spreading of his gospel, and then never to breathe a word about this as we spread that gospel? Are we to thank the Lord for loving us before we loved him, and then never to speak of that love? Must there be constant tension between what we say to God and what we say to men?

It is impossible to be a Calvinist on your knees and an Arminian on your feet. Arminianism is the belief behind the first objection we considered earlier, and it is not true. Another of its errors is that it tells men and women that it is their *response* to the gospel which gives the message power to save. If they will not respond correctly, God can do nothing. God is thus at the mercy of man. Man's will binds God's actions, permitting him to work or preventing him from working. God has never commissioned any man to teach nonsense.

But even many people who are not Arminians never mention election to the unconverted. This raises a number of important questions. Do we honestly believe that we can help people by hiding part of God's Word from them? Is not all of God's Word for all people? Who are we to decide who should hear what? Our Lord Jesus Christ spoke openly about election in front of unbelievers, so why shouldn't we? How tenderly he addressed them in Matthew 11:28-30: 'Come to me, all you who labour and are heavy leaden, and I will give you rest. Take my yoke upon you and learn from me, for I am gentle and lowly in heart, and you will find rest for your souls. For my yoke is easy and my burden is light.' But let us not forget that those words were immediately preceded by words which he spoke to his Father, and which the same people heard: 'I thank you, Father, Lord of heaven and earth, because you have hidden these things from the wise and prudent and have revealed them to babes. Even so, Father, for so it seemed good in your sight. All things have been delivered to me by my Father, and no one knows the Son except the Father. Nor does anyone know the Father except the Son, and he to whom the Son wills to reveal him' (Matt. 11:25-27).

These words of Jesus were also spoken to unbelievers: 'All that the Father gives me will come to me, and the one who comes to me I will by no means cast out' (John 6:37). 'No one can come to me unless the Father who sent me draws him' (John 6:44). 'You do not believe, because you are not of my sheep, as I said to you' (John 10:26).

Many preachers today do not say what Jesus said in this last verse. They say to unbelievers, 'You are not Christ's sheep because you do not believe.' Jesus said exactly the opposite. He made it clear that his hearers did not believe because they were not of his sheep. It is not so that we may *become* sheep that we believe. We believe because we *are* sheep. The sheep are those people whom the Father has given to the Son. Jesus says so in John 10:29. He did not shrink from talking about election to unbelievers. The Christlike thing is to follow his example.

9. If some people are not elect, then they must have been predestined to damnation. How can a God who does that be the loving and merciful God of the Bible?

It is true that God has seen fit to pass some people by. He has hidden spiritual things from them, for it seemed good in his sight (Matt. 11:25). As the great Potter, from the same lump he has made vessels for honour and others for dishonour (Rom. 9:21). The Bible speaks of this as fact.

But these people he has passed by, what are they like? Are they spiritually neutral, neither good nor bad, but somewhere in the middle? Not at all! Without exception, they are willing sinners who every day choose the godless path they tread. They want to be like that. It is not that they are crying out to be saved and God is turning a deaf ear towards them. They are not interested in God and in godliness. They have no intention of repenting. By passing them by, God leaves them where they want to be.

Such people are responsible for their own ruin. If God did not pass them by, but gave them a new nature, they would certainly be saved. But what damns them, in fact, is not God's decision to pass them by. It is their own sin, for which they have no one to blame but themselves.

The proof of the love and mercy of God is that he has not left the whole of mankind to perish in its sin and misery. Out of his mere good pleasure, and from all eternity, he has elected some of these callous rebels to everlasting life. He has decided to save them from their wretchedness by means of a Redeemer. Why he should do this we do not know. Why did he not just consign us all to the hell we deserve? Why did he not pass everybody by? Every man and woman was equally guilty and hopelessly lost. Nobody could have justly complained if God had turned his back on the whole race. But he did not. By sheer grace, he chose a people for himself. This fact shouts out that he is indeed the God of mercy and love that the Bible constantly teaches him to be.

10. The doctrine of election makes assurance impossible

'If I believed in election, I would have to go through life all the time wondering if I was elect or not.' This is how this objection is often expressed. But its fears are groundless.

A believer can ask himself many other questions, besides ones which are directly concerned with election. How is it that I have come to believe, when so many of my family and friends do not? Why do I now feel a sense of kinship with God, indeed of sonship? There can be only one explanation: God is at work in my life. And why would he do such a thing? Again, there can be only one explanation: it is because he has chosen to.

My salvation depends, then, on God. He chose me in grace. And this God is unchangeable. Having set his love on me, will he fail to bring me to heaven? Will he fail to save eternally what he has chosen to save? Will he fail to complete the work he has started?

Once the believer begins to reason in this way, his heart is flooded with new assurance. Do I love God? It is because he loved me first. Have I chosen him? It is because he chose me. My salvation is in God's hands, and not my own. How sure I can be about the future! I am going to glory! I could never be this sure of things if it all depended on me. Yes, 'The godly consideration of predestination, and our election in Christ, is full of sweet, pleasant, and unspeakable comfort to godly persons, and such as feel in themselves the working of the Spirit of Christ' (*Articles of the Church of England,* no.17). How kind God is to have revealed to us the doctrine of election!

There is no objection to the Bible's teaching on election that can stand. In Ephesians 1:3-14 Paul was content to rejoice in it, and so should we be. He taught it to the whole church, including its children (who clearly were present when Ephesians was read out; see 6:1-3). We, too, should not hide it from anybody, under the mistaken notion that people are actually helped by hiding part of God's truth from them.

Perhaps there is somebody reading this book who has not yet turned from sin to God. We have seen that the truth of election provides you with no excuse for remaining as you are. But it does show you the way forward. Salvation is in God's hands. Therefore,

if you would be saved, it is to God you must go. Be sure of this —
if you desire him, it is because he desires you. He undertakes to save
all who call on him. You cannot save yourself, but God saves
eternally all those who come to him through Christ. Cast yourself at
his feet now, and enter into all the blessings of the gospel that we
have been speaking about.

If you are a Christian as you read this, will you not now stop your
reading, and pause to worship? It is because God chose you in Christ
before the foundation of the world that you have come to faith.
Having come to Christ, you have been blessed with every spiritual
blessing in the heavenly places in him. Previously you were not one
of his people, but now you are. Once you were far off; now you are
near. In the past you were damned, but now you are God's child.
You were hell-bound; now you are racing towards your heavenly
inheritance.

> On such love, my soul, still ponder,
>   Love so great, so rich, so free;
> Say, while lost in holy wonder,
>   Why, O Lord, such love to me?
>   Hallelujah!
> Grace shall reign eternally!

                                                   (John Kent, 1766-1843).

4.
Paul's prayer

Please read Ephesians 1:15-23

Our excursion into the doctrine of election was prompted by our study of Ephesians 1:3-14. We come now to see what Paul says next, in 1:15-23. In this passage the apostle tells the Ephesians that from the very moment of their conversion he has been ceaselessly praying for them. He tells us exactly what he has been saying in his prayers. We shall study what he says by asking three questions, and by dividing each of our answers into two parts.

How did Paul know that the Ephesians had become real Christians?

The answer is twofold and is in verse 15. First of all, they had **'faith in the Lord Jesus'**. Faith, as we have already seen in this commentary, has three aspects to it. It is knowing, believing and trusting. A person comes to know what the gospel message is; he believes it to be true; and then he commits himself to what he knows and believes. He relies upon it, by putting himself in the hands of the Christ whom the gospel proclaims.

This is what had happened to the Ephesians. Paul himself had been the instrument by which many of them had come to faith, but many others had believed since he left the city. They knew the truth, assented to it and put their whole weight on the Lord Jesus. He was the object of their faith.

Do you have faith in the Lord Jesus? There is a very easy way to find out. Let me speak to you about your prayers. Why should the great God listen to you? He is holy and you are full of sin. He is of purer eyes than to look upon iniquity, but your heart is filled with it. Why should he pay any attention to what you say to him? On what do you base your hopes of being heard by such a God as this?

If you argue that you pray often, or sincerely, or with energy, and this is why God should listen to you, then you may know that you do not yet have faith in the Lord Jesus Christ. If you rely upon the fact that your life is not as bad as others, or that you are a Bible-reader or churchgoer, this also is a proof that you do not yet have saving faith. Perhaps you think that God must listen to you because of your great need; but even this will not do.

The problem with all this is that you are pointing to something about *you* as the reason why God should hear. Your hopes of being accepted by him are to do with yourself. This is not faith in Christ.

But if all your hopes of being accepted by God are to do with the Lord Jesus Christ, this is the faith of which we are speaking. Do you see yourself as filthy in God's sight? Do you see that there is nothing about you which he will ever find attractive? But do you say in your hearts, 'Yes, but the Lord Jesus Christ has taken upon himself the punishment that I deserve. What is more, his perfect life has been reckoned to my account. It is on the basis of who Christ is and what he has done, that I expect God to receive me. God will not turn away a sinner who comes to him through Christ. It is on him that I rely. I look outside of myself and away to him. I have no other hope than him'?

This is how faith speaks and behaves. It does not think about itself. Its attention is all fixed on Christ. This is how the Ephesians spoke and behaved, and so Paul knew that they had indeed become true Christians.

In addition to their faith in the Lord Jesus, the Ephesians had **'love for all the saints'** (1:15). There are several words for 'love' in Greek, each one having its own range of meanings. In describing the Ephesians' love, Paul uses the word *'agapé'* . What does this mean? It means to seek another person's good, however much it costs me personally. It is a sacrificial word. It is the word usually used of Christ's love for us. It means working for another's welfare, even if I die in the process.

This is the sort of love the Ephesians had. But for whom did they have it? Paul tells us. It was 'for all the saints'. The New Testament speaks of 'saints' in the plural, but never in the singular. The word refers to that whole company of people who have been set apart by

God, for God. They are the ones whom he has chosen in Christ before the foundation of the world, called to faith by the gospel, changed so that they live differently, and kept until they arrive safely in their heavenly home. Only three times are believers called 'Christians' in the New Testament, but they are called 'saints' about sixty times. The Ephesian believers loved every one of them. It was not a love extended to every Christian, except for him, or for her. Every believer at Ephesus loved every believer everywhere.

'Love for all the saints' characterizes every person who has been truly converted. It is a brand-mark which is clearly visible and impossible to remove. Those who are in the family love those who are in the family. If someone does not love those who are in the family of God, it is because he himself is not a member of that family.

This is a fact which, for example, the apostle John stresses again and again: 'He who says he is in the light, and hates his brother, is in darkness until now. He who loves his brother abides in the light, and there is no cause for stumbling in him. But he who hates his brother is in darkness and walks in darkness, and does not know where he is going, because the darkness has blinded his eyes' (1 John 2:9-11). 'We know that we have passed from death to life, because we love the brethren. He who does not love his brother abides in death' (1 John 3:14). 'Beloved, let us love one another, for love is of God; and everyone who loves is born of God and knows God. He who does not love does not know God, for God is love' (1 John 4:7-8). 'If someone says, "I love God," and hates his brother, he is a liar; for he who does not love his brother whom he has seen, how can he love God whom he has not seen? And this commandment we have from him: that he who loves God must love his brother also. Whoever believes that Jesus is the Christ is born of God, and everyone who loves him who begot also loves him who is begotten of him' (1 John 4:20 - 5:1).

Believers are the adopted children of God and they do everything they can to promote the well-being of their new family. They do this, however much it costs them, however inconvenient it is and however much it hurts. They do not consider other Christians as being separate from themselves, but as being part of themselves. They gather with them whenever they can and do not let personal considerations keep them away. They use their tongues to help their brothers and sisters, but not to hurt them. Their homes are open to

one another. How much they enjoy being at table with each other!
They do not hold back their time, talents, or money, if these can be
used in the interest of God's people.

As Paul looked at the Ephesians, this is what he saw in them. Here
were people who relied upon the Lord Jesus Christ for their
salvation, and who loved each other in a practical way. They were
no longer what they used to be. They were not yet what they should
have been, as we shall see later in this epistle. The change was not
perfect, but it was real. Who could have brought about such a
transformation, if it was not God himself? The apostle knew that
these Ephesians really had become Christians.

What did Paul do when he heard of their conversion?

What do you do when you hear of conversions? Paul gave thanks,
as he tells us in verse 16. This was the direct result of his hearing of
their coming to faith, as the 'therefore' in verse 15 makes clear.
When he learned of what was happening at Ephesus, Paul went to
God. He did not do this just once, or even a few times. Again and
again he thanked the Lord, ceaselessly. It was a constant theme in
his prayers.

Of course he gave thanks! Salvation is God's work, as we have
learned dozens of times since starting our study of this epistle. When
a conversion takes place, there is nobody to thank but God. The
whole work of salvation is his, and no human or angel can take the
credit for any part of it. When we hear that somebody has come to
the Lord, congratulations are not in order. We should go to God and
thank him that he is still at work in the world. And as the miracle
which God has brought about is a continuing thing which will go on
until the person concerned leaves this world, our thanks to the Lord
should be unceasing.

Even in Ephesus the Lord Jesus Christ had some sheep! Even in
that city there were people whom God had loved since before time
began! Now he had called them and regenerated them by his Word
alone. Unbelievers had become believers. Many of Satan's follow-
ers had turned to God. God's grace had been seen in action. Lives
had been changed right round. Love reigned among those who had
been ugly and unlovely. What marvellous news! Paul went to his
knees. Wonder of wonders, similar things go on in human lives
today! Who will thank God for it — ceaselessly?

Paul thanked the Lord for the Ephesians. He also prayed for them. **'I ... do not cease to give thanks for you,'** he wrote, **'making mention of you in my prayers'** (1:16). With ceaseless thanksgiving went ceaseless intercession. The Ephesians had entered into a spiritual world and were enjoying spiritual blessings. Paul had seen convincing evidence of this. They were living spiritual lives. But how are such lives nourished and sustained? By spiritual means. There is nothing more spiritual than prayer. Paul was a long way away. Besides, he was in prison. He could not strengthen the Ephesians by his ministry. But he could positively help them by his prayers. He spoke to God about them; and he did not stop speaking to God about them.

There are many people in the world who are new in the faith. Some of them are around us and some are further afield. Some of them we know personally and others we have only heard of. Can they count on our ceaseless prayers? God himself is at work in their lives, but we should not see this as a reason to sit back and do nothing for them. In fact the reverse is true — the fact that God is at work in them is the very best reason to pray for them. That is how Paul saw it. But do we?

What do these recent converts most need? This can be brought into their lives by the prayers of others. The spiritual development of young believers lies with you, with me, with us! Will they ever become what they should be? This depends on how much we pray for them, and whether we pray the right things. We should pray for them on our own and we should pray for them when we are together. There is nothing that a young Christian needs more than that. We do not even need to be with them to sustain them in this way. Who will be bold enough to say that intercessory prayer is a ministry that he cannot exercise? People at home and those who travel to work; the healthy and the bedridden; adults and children — all are able to pray for others. Shall we sin against them by ceasing to pray for them?

What precisely did Paul pray for these new believers?

He addressed himself to the great and glorious God, the same God who had saved them and given them everything in Christ, and he prayed that this giving God would give again (1:17). And what did he ask him to give? He was praying, he told them, that God **'may give to you the spirit of wisdom and revelation in the knowledge**

of him, the eyes of your understanding being enlightened; that you may know ...' (1:17-18).

Wisdom, revelation, knowledge, understanding, enlightenment, 'that you may know...' — this is what Paul asked his heavenly Father to give the Ephesian believers. In short, he was praying that every recent convert would come to know, grasp, understand, realize, take in and *see* certain things.

Paul thus shows us what is the greatest need of every new believer. He did not pray that the Ephesian Christians should be baptized in the Holy Spirit, or that they should be sealed by him. He did not pray that they should come to an experience of 'full surrender', 'entire consecration' or 'victory'. It was not his prayer that they should have exalted experiences, heightened emotions or even, at this stage, some usefulness in the church. His mind was elsewhere.

He prayed that each new believer, and indeed every believer, should *see* certain things. The first need of young Christians is understanding. This understanding must start in the mind and extend to the heart. The new believer needs to see certain facts and truths in such a way that he comes to rejoice in them. They must thrill him to the point that they become convictions by which he will live and die.

If you are a young Christian, above everything else you seek for, seek understanding. If you are tending recent converts, above everything else you give them, give them knowledge. And if you are praying for other believers, pray, with Paul, that they may see, and that they may see two things in particular.

1. That they might know where they are going

In verse 18 Paul prays that the Ephesians **'may know what is the hope of his calling, what are the riches of the glory of his inheritance in the saints...'** Here are two phrases separated by a comma, but they actually refer to the same thing. Let me explain.

Paul wants his readers to know what is the hope of God's calling. Everyone who is a Christian has become one through God's calling. He has heard the gospel with his ears, but also with his heart. The message given to many seems to have been intended only for him. This is because of the work of God's Spirit. Others remained indifferent, but he was convicted of his sin and misery. Others remained confused or untouched, but he came to understand about the person and work of Christ. Others walked away, but he was empowered and persuaded to choose the Son of God and to trust him alone, as he was freely presented in the gospel.

This experience is termed 'calling'. It is what makes a believer into a believer, and it ushers him into a world of hope. 'Hope' in the Bible is not something you fondly long for but are never certain to have. It is a word used of certainties that we do not yet possess. The Christian's hope is the hope of death in communion with Christ. It is the hope of the resurrection of the just. It is the hope of acquittal at the judgement seat. It is the hope of heaven — of at last being where there is no sin and sorrow, but only holiness and happiness. It is the hope of getting home safely.

Paul wants these young Christians to understand exactly what is the hope into which God's call has brought them. He wants them to know all about 'the riches of the glory of his inheritance in the saints'. We are looking forward to going home to glory. And God is looking forward to having us there! We shall be immeasurably rich by being there. God will consider himself rich by having us there! We, God's adopted children, shall have our inheritance; that inheritance is glorious, because it is God's. And he shall have *his* inheritance — us.

When did you last pray that the new believers you know would see where they are going? We live in a pleasure-loving age. It tells us that what matters is what is going on *now*. But God's Word does not talk like that. There are many things to enjoy in the present, certainly; but there are also sufferings to bear, and a cross to carry. But there are better things ahead! Sadly, the modern-day philosophy of existentialism has filtered right down to the pew of the church. Even Christians are more and more taken up with the here and now. But Paul says to the Ephesians, 'I am praying that you will have a different and grander vision; that you will see where you are certainly going; that you will be clear about what your ultimate destination is. I want you to know where God's calling is going to lead you.'

In this awful world, Christians sometimes become very disheartened. They often wonder if they can keep going. But when they catch a glimpse of the Celestial City all their courage returns! They are no longer ashamed to be different from the people around them. They walk through Vanity Fair with new confidence, for they remember that they are going somewhere better and eternal.

If you lose sight of heaven, you will quickly be swamped by other things. Materialism will wash over you and your Christian life will sink. Only heavenly-mindedness can stop this happening. We are to set our affections on things above. We are to think about bigger things. When we do this, we have no trouble enjoying all that is good and helpful in this present life, for nothing now diverts us from our greatest priorities. How could we ever want to be like the people of the world, with such riches before us?

2. *That they might know what has happened to them*

Paul talks about this in verses 19-23. He tells us that the power of God has reached down into this world. Writing in Greek, Paul uses four different words for 'power' in verse 19, to bring home to us how great this power is.

What has this power done? It has entered the rock-hewn tomb of Joseph of Arimathea and has snatched out of it the body of him of whom God had said, 'This is my beloved Son, in whom I am well pleased' (Matt. 3:17). It has raised him from the dead. During forty days, by many infallible proofs, our Lord showed himself to be alive. Then his Father exalted him even more by bringing him back to the glory which he had enjoyed before he came to earth. But he re-entered it as a man. He continued to be what he always was — God. But he had become what he was not before — man. And it was bearing the human name of Jesus that he returned to the glory which he had had with the Father before the world began.

Surrounding the throne of Jehovah are innumerable ranks of adoring angels. The glorified Man did not take his place with the principalities, nor did he align himself with powers, thrones or dominions. He swept past them all and ascended above the very highest name to be named, not only in this age but also in that which is to come. There, where only God is, and only God has a right to be, he took his seat! The Father's power took him there, and it was there that the Father's welcome awaited him. He has put all things under his feet.

There is nowhere that Jesus Christ does not rule. He is over all. But for whose benefit does he rule the universe? Verse 22 gives us the answer. He does it for the church. He reigns in order to further the interests of believers. We are down here on the earth, but our Lord does not stand aloof from us. We are his body, and he is our head. Christ and his people are bound together by an inextricable link. We belong to each other, and his life is our life.

We are already touching on the teaching of verse 23. But what does the apostle mean when he says that the church, Christ's body, is **'the fulness of him who fills all in all'**?

He means that our Lord Jesus Christ regards himself as incomplete until every person whom the Father gave him has been joined to him in living faith. But there is more to say than that. How is our Lord represented and expressed in this world? It is by his church. And that church is intended to be a full expression of him. Of whom? Of him 'who fills all in all'; of him who reigns over the whole universe, and whom the whole creation will at last acknowledge to be Lord alone; of him who, by his Spirit, is present everywhere, and whose name is the only one which will be praised eternally.

But why is Paul telling us all this? These truths are wonderful, but isn't the apostle getting off his subject? Not at all. Paul's point is that the power which raised the Lord Jesus Christ from the lowest place to the highest, the very power which sustains the wonderful relationship that exists between the ascended Christ and his people — *that* power is the power which has worked in you as a Christian. Paul is praying that his fellow-Christians might really see **'what is the exceeding greatness of his power towards us who believe, according to the working of his mighty power which he worked in Christ ...'** (1:19-20).

The power that did all this for Christ is the very same power which works in a man, woman or child at conversion! Conversion is a spiritual resurrection, as we shall see in the next chapter. What is dead comes to life. It is a complete and radical spiritual transformation. Those who are spiritually dead, and therefore insensitive, come to spiritual life and enjoyment. But the dead cannot raise themselves. An outside power must do it. And the outside power which converts us is exactly the same power that resurrected and exalted the Lord Jesus Christ!

What power it takes to bring about a single conversion! No wonder we cannot convert anybody. But the new believer does not always realize what has happened to him. He sees things he could not see before, but he does not know why. Other things he sees in a

new light, and he is baffled by it. He does not understand why his
affections, desires and choices are different. Everything is new. It is
as if he had been made all over again!

We should tell the new Christian what has happened to him. Paul
does this in chapter 2. But it is more important to pray that he will
grasp the full truth of it. Then he will be overwhelmed — the very
power which raised Christ from the dead has been stretched out
again to raise *him* from the dead! Once he even begins to take this
in, the believer is filled with wonder. He understands what conversion is, and how great it is. He is also staggered by God's personal
interest in him.

Those who see conversion as a thing of small wonder are always
stunted in their spiritual growth. Some of them even begin to chase
after dramatic post-conversion experiences, believing them to be
greater than conversion itself. All who have ever done this have
ended up with a deformed view of the gospel. Nothing goes right in
their spiritual lives after this. They stop asking, 'Why me?' They
cease to be filled with amazed thanks at the way the great God has
worked in their lives. By devaluing conversion, they devalue the
power of God. Their minds are taken off the death, resurrection and
exaltation of Christ to something else. They are thus easy prey for
any error that may attempt to seduce them.

How we should pray that young believers might be spared from
that! They will be, if we pray for them as Paul prayed for the
Ephesians. Imagine what the outcome would be. From the earliest
days of their Christian lives, converts would be filled with a never-
dying expectancy of heaven, and with astonishment at the great
work that God has done in their lives. Spiritual conversation would
come from their lips and spiritual priorities would be evident in their
lives. They would talk of Christ and live for him.

Do you want to see the church filled with Christians like that?
The proof will be that you make Paul's prayer for new believers the
model for your own ceaseless praying.

5.
Once dead — now alive

Please read Ephesians 2:1-10

In the first chapter of his letter, the apostle Paul has told the Ephesians that he is praying for them. One of the things he has been praying is that they might clearly see what has happened to them. But he doesn't just pray this for them. He decides to tell them — and this is what chapter 2 is about.

If you are a believer at all, it is because something has happened to you! Once you were dead, but now you are alive (2:1-10). Once you were cut off, but now you have been brought near (2:11-22). It is the first of these sections that we come to look at now. The apostle will tell you what you were, what you are, and what made the difference.

What you were (2:1-3)

1. You were dead (2:1)

You **'were dead in trespasses and sins'**. Think back to your unconverted years. Every day God spoke to you through his creation. The sky above your head and the ground beneath your feet declared the eternal power and Godhead of the invisible Lord. In addition to this, God spoke to you through your conscience. You had a sense of right and wrong, a sense of law. You knew in your heart of hearts that there was a Lawgiver and, therefore, that there would also be a final judgement. You could not escape the speaking voice.

God spoke to many of you even more directly than this. You heard his Word in Sunday School, or church, or elsewhere. He spoke and spoke, but you did not hear. That was the experience of us all before we were converted. We trespassed, repeatedly violating God's law. We sinned, constantly failing to come up to his standard. And we didn't care. It meant nothing to us. We were dead in trespasses and sins.

I shall never forget the day when one of my best friends died. I was a late teenager at the time. Others came running up from the fields to tell me that he had dropped dead there. A Land Rover took his body to his home, where it was laid down in the front room. The family asked if I would like to go and see him. Two nights earlier I had spent a whole evening with him, talking of the ways and work of God. Now I was alone with him again. My first reaction was to speak to him, but the prostrate body did not answer. I spoke again. There was no reply. He could neither see, nor hear, nor talk, nor move; nor could he even want to. He certainly could not bring himself back to life. He was dead.

This is precisely the picture that Paul uses. God spoke to us, and spoke to us again; but we were dead. We did not listen to him, and we did not want to listen to him. We did not hear him, desire him, or choose him. We could not do it. The truth was announced to us but it was impossible for us to see it. It was as if there were no divine voice at all. And this is how it is with all unconverted people. Even when they are exposed to all the external influences to which Christians are exposed, it means nothing to them. God's Word meets with silence. There is no response. I was like that, and so were you. You were dead.

2. You were disobedient (2:2-3)

With shame we remember how we **'once walked'**. Although spiritually dead, we lived our lives in active opposition to God. Dead and unresponsive as far as he and his Word were concerned, we walked in a certain way, and our lives were going in a definite direction. We **'walked according to the course of this world'**. We were going the same way as everybody else. God was not in our lives and we did not want him to be. We walked with the crowd, but we didn't walk with him.

We lived as we wanted to. But why did we want to live that way? It was because of a spiritual power which is still making people disobedient to God today. When we look at the unconverted, we cannot have a 'holier-than-thou' attitude. We used to be unconverted, all of us. We were once non-Christians. **'We all once conducted ourselves in the lusts of our flesh, fulfilling the desires of the flesh and of the mind.'** 'The flesh' means fallen human nature. It is the word the Bible uses to speak of abject selfishness. It was that which once governed us completely. All that mattered to us was our own self-centred world of indulgence, ambition and pleasure. Our bodies did what they wanted to do, and our minds thought what they wanted to think, whether God was pleased or not. He was not in all our thoughts. We were godless and subject to another power. The devil motivated us without drawing attention to himself, just as he still does with unconverted people everywhere.

The Christian church often speaks of 'the world, the flesh and the devil'. Now we see why. 'The world' refers to human society operating without reference to God. We were previously in the world. 'The flesh' is human nature in rebellion against God. We committed widely varying sins before our conversion, but human nature was behind them all, so we were not as different from each other as we sometimes think. 'The devil' is the sworn enemy of God. We were on his side, rejecting God's rule over us. I was disobedient. You were disobedient.

3. You were damned (2:3)

You **'were by nature children of wrath, just as the others'**. 'Wrath' is anger in action. Angry outbursts were a sad feature of our unconverted days. Bad temper is always found where people live for themselves. But that is not what Paul is talking about here.

When a sinner is angry, his sin will always taint that anger. God is holy. His anger is therefore pure. He is furious with all that is impure. Of course he is, for sin is a contradiction of his nature and, besides, it is sin which has spoiled his creation. Everything was good, so very good, until sin came along.

Sin does not exist in the abstract, and God is not angry with sin in the abstract. It is sinners who sin. They do what they do because they are what they are. God is angry with sin and he is angry with those who commit sin. He is actively angry with sinners. Living under his wrath is such a marked characteristic of their lives that they are described here as 'children of wrath'. It is the distinctive feature of their lives. They live the whole of their life with God's anger hanging over them. They wake in the morning, pass through the day and go to sleep at night with God's wrath over them. Because of their sin he is never for them and always against them.

'We were like that,' says Paul. '"The others", that is non-Christians, are still like that. But let us not forget that we were previously like that. And we were like that by nature.'

Paul is reminding us that we were born that way. We did not *become* sinners. We have always been sinners, which is why we sin. Our parents were sinners before us. Only our first parents knew what it was like to be without sin. But when they sinned, we sinned in them; and when they fell, we fell with them. Nobody may say that he is less guilty than they were. Our nature is corrupt and we have repeated their sin every day of our lives. This corruption of our nature is called 'original sin' and it is a fact of human existence. Even babies are often selfishly angry. From birth we have lived for ourselves. All that humanity is today, we once were.

How we should tremble as we think about this! For how many years were we disobedient, unresponsive and hell-bound? At any moment God could have stopped our breath and sent us screaming into conscious everlasting punishment. But he didn't! It was what we deserved. We daringly provoked him as our rebellion and unbelief increased by the minute. He did us good, 'gave us rain from heaven and fruitful seasons, filling our hearts with food and gladness' (Acts 14:17), but we did not lift our hearts to him. How kind he was! How rich in mercy! There was no wrong in his anger. All the fault was ours. I was damned. You were damned.

What you are (2:4-7)

1. You are alive! (2:5)

'Even when we were dead in trespasses, [God] made us alive together with Christ (by grace you have been saved).' If you are a Christian, you have experienced a resurrection — an event of such significance that the Bible calls it 'the first resurrection'.

That day when they laid my friend's body on his living-room floor, I would have given all I possessed to be able to speak a word which would have raised him to life. I spoke to him, but my words had no power.

How different it is with God! Chapter 1 showed us that his power wrenched his Son from the grave and raised him to an endless life. That very same power is what reached down to bring about our conversion. It was a resurrection indeed! The Word we had heard a thousand times before, we heard as if for the very first time. Others had often spoken to us about the glories of Christ, but now it meant something to us. They had warned us of our danger, but we had felt no danger. They had pointed out our sin, but we had no sense of sin. But then everything changed! Our souls sprang to life.

If I could have been heard by my dead friend that day, he would have got up and come to me. He would have left the room to embrace his wife and family. It would have been wonderful to see such movement. Movement is the evidence of resurrection. When spiritual resurrection takes place, we move to Christ and embrace him as he is so plainly held out to us in the gospel.

Verse 5 tells us that God made us alive *together with Christ.* Union with Christ is a central part of the gospel's teaching. If you are a believer, I have something wonderful to tell you. When the Lord Jesus Christ died on the cross, his death was reckoned to be your death, which is why all your sins are considered to have been punished. Not only so, but his resurrection was reckoned to be your resurrection. You were reckoned to have risen from the dead at the same moment. This is already seen in your spiritual resurrection. It is only a matter of time before it will also be seen in your bodily resurrection at the end of the world. Such resurrection comes to you through your union with Christ, in whom you were chosen. You are alive.

2. You are accepted (2:6)

'**[God] raised us up together, and made us sit together in the heavenly places in Christ Jesus.**' Where is the Lord Jesus Christ now? After his resurrection he walked the earth for nearly six weeks, giving his disciples further teaching. Then, while they watched, he physically ascended and a cloud received him out of their sight. He returned to the right hand of majesty, and that is where he is now.

But we who believe are united to Christ! Where he is, we are! Raised with him, we are seated with him 'in the heavenly places in Christ Jesus'. That is why you can pray. You are not reckoned to be an outsider — you are in Christ, and all that God sees Christ to be, he reckons you to be. You are on the inside, with immediate access to the throne. This is also why death does not hurt the Christian believer. It has lost its sting. We are already spiritually seated in heaven. When we die, our spirits have no voyage to make. They are already in heaven. That is where they belong, by virtue of their union with Christ, and they cannot be turned away.

This leads us directly to the next point.

3. You are assured (2:7)

God has raised and accepted you, **'that in the ages to come he might show the exceeding riches of his grace in his kindness towards us in Christ Jesus'**. Soon this earth and universe, as we know them now, will be gone. The devil, and all who have remained on his side, will be in hell. There will be a new heaven and a new earth in which only righteousness will be found. This renewed universe will be inhabited, not only by God and his holy angels, but also by Christian believers. We are talking about certainties. Where Christ is, there he has promised we shall be also.

By nature we are sinners, defiled in God's sight. What we used to be will never be forgotten. Nor will it be forgotten how sinners come to be in a place where only holiness is found. It is all through Christ and their union with him. Throughout endless ages the universe will be in perpetual astonishment — sinners are with God in his home! All that God is and has done will be admired in that everlasting glory. But shining brighter than all will be his abounding grace, seen in the kindness he has shown, through Christ, towards sinners.

God's purpose in redeeming us is to exhibit his own glory. If just one redeemed sinner fails to arrive in God's dwelling-place, God's glory will be tarnished. When a creature seeks his own glory, it is a sin, for he is only a creature. But God must glorify himself, because he *is* God. He cannot glorify himself in the way that he has decreed, unless he brings to heaven every person whom he has chosen, redeemed and called. Every true believer will be there! God will 'show the exceeding riches of his grace in his kindness towards us in Christ Jesus'.

What made the difference (2:4-5,8-10)

You have seen what you were. You know what you are. What made the difference? Three words will help us to remember.

1. God (2:4-5,10)

There you were in your spiritual deadness. Who gave you life? It was certainly not yourself. It was God. This work is a divine work, a work you could not do. You could not even choose God, because the will is the servant of your nature, and your nature was fallen and spiritually dead. God was not compelled to give you spiritual life. But he did: **'But God who is rich in mercy, because of his great love with which he loved us, even when we were dead in trespasses, made us alive together with Christ (by grace you have been saved)'** (2:4-5). What love — undeserved and unsought; what grace!

Why are you today what you are? Because God has been at work. **'For we are his workmanship, created in Christ Jesus for good works, which God prepared beforehand that we should walk in them'** (2:10). All men and women are his creatures. You are his new creature, made anew in Jesus Christ. It is God's everlasting decree which has decided that your life should be changed right round, that you should live differently, that you should spend your days doing things which God considers pleasing. As long as he has been God, it has been his will that you should be a new person in Christ, and that you should live accordingly. You know what you were and you know what you are. You can take no credit for the change. It was beyond your power. 'But God ...'

> Thank you, Lord, for saving my soul;
> Thank you, Lord, for making me whole;
> Thank you, Lord, for giving to me
>   Thy great salvation so rich and free.

2. *Grace* (2:4,5,8)

You were just the same as others, as we have seen. The reason for your salvation, then, does not lie in anything you are, but in what *he* is. It is **'because of his great love with which he loved us'** (2:4). It was nothing in us, but what is within God, that moved him to save us. He is **'rich in mercy'** (2:4).

What is mercy? And what is the difference between mercy and grace? An illustration told by the great children's evangelist Hudson Pope will make it clear. Some boys broke panes of glass in his greenhouse and he was able to speak to the culprits. He explained that he could deal with them by law or by grace. To deal with them by law would mean taking them to the police station, to be prosecuted and punished. But he had decided against that. They deserved punishment, but they would not be getting it. That was mercy, he said. Instead, they would receive from him what they did not deserve. He would treat them with kindness, give them his friendship, and pay for the glass himself. That, he said, was grace.

Mercy is not receiving what you deserve. Grace is receiving what you don't deserve. God's anger has not fallen on us, for he is 'rich in mercy' (2:4). Instead, he has heaped upon us blessing after blessing — spiritual resurrection, unreserved acceptance into his presence and a certain place in heaven. He has not simply pardoned us and left us in a neutral condition. He has adopted us and called us his. **'By grace you have been saved ... for by grace you have been saved'** (2:5,8).

3. *Gift* (2:8-10)

In order not to miss the full impact of what the apostle is saying, we need to meditate more fully on verses 8-10: **'For by grace you have been saved through faith, and that not of yourselves; it is the gift of God, not of works, lest anyone should boast. For we are his workmanship, created in Christ Jesus for good works, which God prepared beforehand that we should walk in them.'**

All that Jesus Christ has done for his people becomes theirs in experience by means of faith. Faith, as we have seen more than once, is knowing, believing and trusting. These are things that men and women *do*. When they receive salvation, they are not passive. They are active. But this does not mean they have contributed something to their salvation.

There is a lot of misunderstanding on this point today. Every repentant sinner knows that he has no good works to bring to God. He can do nothing to earn or deserve God's favour. But sometimes preachers give the impression that although we cannot satisfy God's demands, he is pleased when we come to him with our faith. The idea is left that Christ has done everything to save us; we must just contribute faith. Everything else is represented as coming from God, but faith is spoken of as if it came from us.

This is not the way it is at all. It is true that we exercise faith when we receive the gospel, but from where does that faith come? Verses 8-10 tell us. The whole grace-through-faith experience, in its entirety, is God's gift to us. None of it has its origin in us. If it did, we would have at least something to congratulate ourselves on. We would not have much to be proud about, but we would have *something*. But Paul rejects this completely. There is nothing at all on which we can flatter ourselves. The grace-through-faith way of saving us, all of it, is **'not of yourselves; it is the gift of God, not of works, lest anyone should boast'**.

Imagine offering a corpse a present. The corpse comes to life, stretches out a hand and dances away, clasping the gift. Could the former corpse congratulate himself on that? Would he feel he had made any contribution to his joy? Would he not, rather, give all the credit to the one who spoke the life-giving word? Would not his praise be doubled when he found out that the life-giver and the present-giver were one and the same person?

Salvation and faith are not two separate things. The act of trusting Christ is part of salvation. Salvation in its totality is God's gift of grace to us. It follows that faith is his gift. How is it that you could not believe, but you do now? You neglected him for years and years, but then you came to trust him. What made the difference? Did you suddenly improve? No; God was gracious to you. He gave salvation to you. It was sheer grace that brought you to believe and receive.

And how is it that you have a completely changed life? How we all love to repeat it: **'We are his workmanship, created in Christ Jesus for good works, which God prepared beforehand that we should walk in them'** (2:10). Other people think that we live good lives *in order to be* saved. How wrong they are! We live good lives *because* we *are* saved. We hold out no hope of being saved by works. But one of the reasons for which God has saved us is that we should live differently on this earth. He has put each of his children in a certain set of circumstances where there are a whole series of good acts to be done. He wants them to set about doing them. This is as much part of his eternal plan as all the other things we have spoken about. He has made us new; and he has done it that we might live as new people in the very place where we find ourselves today. He who has decided our eternal destination has certainly decided our earthly route.

As we close this section, may I speak very pointedly but affectionately to every reader of this book? Is there an unconverted person who has read this far? You have seen that salvation is entirely God's work. Man has no part in it. It must be clear to you now that you cannot save yourself. Only God can do that. Nobody but the Lord Jesus Christ provides all that you need. Salvation is complete, but it is entirely in the hands of God. You cannot stay as you are without perishing, and there is nowhere to go except to God. Fall before him now and cry, 'God be merciful to me, a sinner!' If you do that, it will be because God has already given you faith. You will know that you are spiritually alive, accepted by God, and assured of final glory!

And what shall I say to those who are already believers? God has done his wonderful work in you and you cannot take one ounce of credit for it. You were once unresponsive, ungodly and damned. You are now resurrected, seated in heavenly places in Christ Jesus, and about to begin an eternity of perfect praise where your theme will be the mercy and grace of God. Thanks be to him for ever remembering the dust of the earth!

We shall praise him in heaven, so shall we not praise him on earth? But our words are so poor. Yes, but we may also praise him by our lives. We have been 'created in Christ Jesus for good works'. Let us get on with them. Is there a better way to show that we who were once dead are now alive?

6.
Once separated — now united

Please read Ephesians 2:11-22

In this section the apostle Paul continues to tell new believers what has happened to them. In verses 1-10 he told them that once they were dead, but now they are alive. In verses 11-22 he tells them that once they were separated, but now they are united. It is a passage which teaches us two straightforward lessons.

We must never forget what we once were (2:11-12)

Do you? Or do you take time to sit down and reflect on what you might have been if the Lord had not saved you? Where would you be today if he had not stepped into your life by his grace? What sort of company might you have been keeping? What might you have been doing? What sort of character would you have? What would be your thoughts about life and death? What scale of values would you be living by and what ambitions would you be nursing? How would your family be run? What would you find pleasurable? This would be largely speculation. But there is no speculation about what we once were, and this is something we are commanded to remember (2:11).

And what were we? Verses 11-12 refresh our memory. To understand verse 11 we must recall that most of Paul's readers were Gentiles, just like most people reading this book. The Jews looked down on them. They called them 'Gentile dogs', or just **'Gentiles'**, saying it with a sneer on their lips. They called themselves **'the Circumcision'**. On the body of every one of their boys they put the covenant sign which declared that God had had unique dealings with their nation. They called the rest of the world **'the Uncircumcision'** and scornfully despised them: 'They are not the people of God, the people with whom God has made his covenant.' Paul reminds his readers of these things. As far as the Jews were concerned, they were beyond the pale; they were unwelcome outsiders.

Paul's reminder continues in verse 12. Former days must not be forgotten. **'At that time you were without Christ,'** he continues. All the Jews carried in their hearts some expectancy of the Messiah, or Christ, as Greek-speakers called him. 'But you didn't. You never gave him a thought. And when he did come, you had nothing to do with him. Christ was in no sense part of your world.' And, today, we have to admit that the same thing was true of us. Sometimes his name was on our lips — as a swear-word. But we were separate from him. He was not a factor or reality in our lives.

Also at that time, continues Paul, you were **'aliens from the commonwealth of Israel'** (2:12). Walking in this world is a nation to whom God has revealed himself. To that nation he gave his Word. He spoke at various times and in different ways. 'But you were not members of that nation. You were not part of that special people.'

'At that time you were ... strangers from the covenants of promise' (2:12). The Old Testament reports how God made repeated covenants with Israel. These covenants were filled with promises. Who were the promises for? They were for those with whom the covenant was made. God's pledges were for Hebrew ears. Gentiles did not belong to the privileged people. Generally speaking, they did not even know that God had made such promises. If they did, they rightly concluded it was nothing to do with them. They were outsiders. God's comforting words to Abraham, Isaac and Jacob were not for them.

This being so, the Gentiles had **'no hope'** (2:12). The Jews had hope, for they were expecting the Messiah. Their hope was real, for the covenants overflowed with divine promises. But their hope was unshared.

'No hope!' What profoundly empty words! Is there any more eloquent way of describing our unconverted years? We had no hope beyond this life, and no hope in it. We knew that God existed but fostered no hope of ever finding him. We realized that the world's treasures were but tinsel but nursed no hope of discovering anything better. Our present existence had no meaning and we could not give it one. Death was a blank finality which we looked at with despair. Even our bright moments wore a shroud. They can have no enduring beauty where there is no hope.

Being 'without Christ' we were **'without God in the world'** (2:12). We knew about him. Conscience, creation and Scripture are how he made us aware of him, as we have already seen several times in these pages. But we did not know him. We lived in his world without him. He was not a living, bright reality to us. Some of us felt after him, in various religions, false Christianity and philosophy. But we did not find him there. We were orphans. We did not have him as our Father, as we do today. In him we lived, and moved and had our being, but we did not enjoy him. He could just as well have been a million miles away.

All this is what we once were and we are never to forget it. Only now do we see how horrendous it all was. We were separate in two ways — we were separated from God, and we were separated from his people. Countless numbers of people in today's world are still like that. Verses 11-12, which so graphically describe our unconverted misery, are a clear account of the awfulness of being non-Christians. They have no hope! They went to bed that way last night, and they have woken up like that this morning. They know that God is, but to them he is the unknown God. They are living and dying without Christ and without a personal knowledge of any spiritual privilege. If it were not for God's grace we would still be as they are. 'There, but for the grace of God, go I.' We must never forget what we once were.

2. We must never forget what we now are (2:13-22)

You will remember that a chief concern of Paul's letter to the Ephesians is to speak to us about spiritual blessings. Christian men and women must realize how rich they are! This section is devoted to driving this home. It uses a number of pictures which are easy to understand, and yet the concepts behind them are mind-stretching.

1. *One nation* (2:13-18)

Paul has been speaking to us about what we were 'at that time' (2:12). He opens this section with the words: **'But now ...'** Every true Christian can remember what he was, and can compare it with what he is now. He or she can say, 'Things are different now; something has happened to me.' Can you? How sad it is that so many people who believe themselves to be Christians cannot use this sort of language! They have never had a decided conversion. They are unable to speak of any change that has taken place. Such people are not yet true believers.

What the Ephesians had been, and what they had become, could be contrasted. **'But now in Christ Jesus you who were once far off have been made near by the blood of Christ'** (2:13). 'I have reminded you', says Paul, 'that you were once cut off, both from God and from his people. This is no longer the case. Those days are over. Now that you are in Christ Jesus, everything has changed. It is the spilling of his blood that has brought you near!' The apostle is highlighting what he taught us in chapter 1. Every spiritual blessing is ours on the simple condition of being 'in Christ'. Everything in this realm comes to us by the way of the cross. Nothing comes to us any other way. It was all procured for us when the Son of God bled.

It was not just that the Lord Jesus Christ made peace. He *is* our peace (2:14). We understand this well enough with respect to our separation from God. Our sins were put to Christ's account, and his righteousness was put to ours. But Paul has more than that in mind here. Reconciliation has been made horizontally, as well as vertically. In fact, this is the chief thought of verse 14.

What does the verse say? **'For he himself is our peace, who has made both one, and has broken down the middle wall of division between us.'** Paul is thinking about the temple at Jerusalem. It was a structure that emphasized the difference between Jews and Gentiles. The Gentiles were allowed into the outer courtyard of the temple, but no further. They could admire the Jews' privileges from outside, but could not enter into them. A small wall marked the limit. Warning notices on it told all Gentiles that they went any further on pain of death. Jews passed freely by, but Gentiles had to stop. The small wall announced to all that some were welcome and others were excluded.

That wall no longer exists. This is what Paul is teaching. The division of the world into Jews and Gentiles has ended at the cross. There is no place to which a Jew can go to which a Gentile cannot also go. It is the Lord Jesus Christ who has made the difference. All the privileges which were previously reserved for the Jews alone, are now available to the Gentiles, through Christ.

We understand well enough how the cross reconciles sinners to God. But how, precisely, does it bring about reconciliation between Jew and Gentile? Paul's answer is in verse 15. The Lord Jesus Christ has **'abolished in his flesh the enmity, that is, the law of commandments contained in ordinances, so as to create in himself one new man from the two, thus making peace'.** But what does that mean?

Do you remember the ceremonial law given to the Jews in the Old Testament? It declared certain things clean, while others were unclean. Certain foods defiled you, while others could be enjoyed. If you touched certain things, a dead body for example, you became ceremonially impure. You had to go through a sometimes complicated purifying process before you could take your place in society again. Certain days were holy while others were not special in any way. There were sacrifices and rituals, garments, processions, feast days and a thousand other laws to be observed all the time. The Jew could not live a day without thinking about it all.

It was that ceremonial law which was the source of the hostility between Jew and Gentile. The Jew considered the Gentile to be unclean. The Gentile found the Jew arrogant. He saw him as someone who believed himself to be superior. The ceremonial law was the cause of hostility, tension and bitterness.

Why did God give this law to his ancient people? It was a preparation for the coming of Christ. Everything in it was full of significance, speaking in some way or other of the Saviour who was to come. But when Christ came, there was no longer any need for the ceremonial law. When he died on the cross, all the previous sacrifices became obsolete. When he entered into heaven as our great High Priest there was no need for the Levitical priesthood to continue. Now that he cleanses us by his blood and indwells us by his Spirit, all that ceremonial business about defilement and purification is redundant. There is no longer any place for it. It serves no further purpose. It must be discarded.

By his death, our Lord Jesus Christ has destroyed the cause of hostility between Jew and Gentile. He has 'abolished in his flesh the enmity'. Salvation is given to both Jew and Gentile alike on the basis of Christ's blood and righteousness. Whether it be a Jew or Gentile that comes to Christ, they are both cleansed by the same blood. They both have the same righteous life reckoned to their account. They are indwelt by the same Spirit and, for their access into God's presence, depend on the same priesthood. No barrier now divides them from each other. It is the Lord Jesus Christ who made peace between them. A new nation is to be found on earth, composed of believing Jews and Gentiles. The old way of dividing people into these two categories is now out of date and finished for ever. But there is still a division of the human race into two. Some people are members of that new nation, and some are not.

Verse 15 could not have been clearer. But even when things are as clear as can be, we are still slow to grasp them. This is why Paul writes verse 16. It does not tell us anything new. It simply drives home what we have just learned.

Christ did what he did for both Jew and Gentile **'that he might reconcile them both to God in one body through the cross, thereby putting to death the enmity'** (2:16). Both are restored to fellowship with God in the same way — by the same cross, by the same broken body, by the same sacrifice. This being so, there is no reason at all for them to remain separated from each other. The ceremonial law is dead and buried, and so therefore is the ill-will and antagonism which once kept Jew and Gentile apart.

Why, then, is it that some Christians still want to keep the ceremonial law alive? Why, for example, do supposedly Christian travel agents encourage us to go to Palestine to join with Jews there in the celebration of the Feast of Tabernacles? And why do some Christian leaders still continue to talk of 'Hebrew Christians' and 'Gentile Christians'? Since Christ came, there are no more feast days to keep, and the world, much less the church, is no longer divided into Jews and Gentiles. There are no 'Hebrew Christians' and there are no 'Gentile Christians'. Christ has created 'in himself one new man from the two' (2:15), having reconciled them 'both to God in one body'. There are just 'Christians'.

In Christ, both Jew and Gentile make up a single nation. **'And he came and preached peace to you who were afar off and to those who were near. For through him we both have access by one Spirit to the Father'** (2:17-18). There are not two different ways of salvation, one for the Jews and the other for the Gentiles. The same Preacher came to both, and both have access to God in precisely the same manner.

We know when the Lord Jesus Christ preached to the Jews, 'to those who were near'. But when did he preach to those 'who were afar off'; that is, to the Gentiles in general and to the Ephesians in particular?

We understand this when we understand the nature of New Testament preaching. Jesus never visited Ephesus and the Ephesians never saw him in the flesh. And yet he preached there! He did it through the preaching of Paul and those who came after him. The physical lips which announced the message were not those which spoke in Nazareth. But where the gospel is being faithfully proclaimed, there Christ is speaking. The New Testament insists on this point. Those whom Christ sends are to be received as if he himself were present; those who reject such messengers reject him. 'He who is sent is as he who sends,' says an old Jewish proverb.

So Jesus Christ himself preached at Ephesus. He was personally addressing them in the gospel that Paul announced. This is what gave the message its authority, just as it is today. Those who reject the gospel are not rejecting the preacher who brings it, but God's Son himself. Even when the divine message is proclaimed by stumbling lips, it is still Jesus Christ who is speaking to the hearers. What a great responsibility this lays upon them! How they should tremble!

The Lord has not restricted his message to either Jew or Gentile. He has preached, and he preaches, to those who are afar off; and he has preached, and continues to preach, to those who are near. Both have access to God by the same Spirit — the Spirit who gave them repentance, faith in Christ, and a heart to pray. Gentiles who believe are not outside Israel and Jews who believe have not left Israel. Together, they *are* Israel — the true Israel of God.

This is very important teaching. In the Old Testament, the whole of God's true Israel was found in the earthly nation that bore that name. Not everyone in that nation was a true Israelite. The vast majority did not walk with the Lord in any personal way. They were Israelites only in name. But the few true believers that existed were all Israelites. God's true Israel was found only in earthly Israel.

This is no longer the case. Today, God's true Israel is found both in earthly Israel and out of it. In fact, most true Israelites are not physical Jews. There is only one Israel. There has only ever been one. But membership of it is no longer restricted to those in the earthly nation. Believing Gentiles are no longer outside Israel; they are not strangers to the covenants; they are actually part and parcel of the people of God. Together with believing Jews, they make up one new nation. Paul gives similar teaching to this in Romans chapters 2,4 and 9-11. He is giving it to us here so that we may never forget what we now are.

2. *One building* (2:19-22)

What you were, **'you are no longer'** (2:19). Here, once again, is the Christian language of which we spoke earlier. Believers can constantly call to mind that they are 'no longer' what they used to be. The Lord's people talk that way, but other people cannot.

Building on what he has just said, Paul tells the Ephesians (and us) that they **'are no longer strangers and foreigners, but fellow-citizens with the saints and members of the household of God'** (2:19).

Here are two sets of opposites. No longer strangers, they have become fellow-citizens with the saints. No longer foreigners, they have become members of the household of God.

Paul was writing in the first century. In that ancient world, two sorts of people lived within a city's walls. There were those who came from elsewhere but had no right of residence, and no say in the city's affairs. They were tolerated, because of the businesses they ran. The word used for these people is the word translated 'strangers' in verse 19. Then, of course, there were the citizens who belonged there by right. As far as the true Israel of God is concerned, we are no longer 'strangers', but as much citizens of it as were Abraham, Isaac, Jacob, Moses or David. Gentiles who believe are in no way inferior to them. They are fellow-citizens with the saints.

The second pair of opposites speaks of a family. Under the same roof are sometimes found family members, but also others who are outside the family circle. These others live there, but they do not belong by right, nor do they enjoy the closeness of bond which the family members have with each other. Gentile believers are no longer like those outsiders. They are as much members of the family as anyone else. Chapter 1 told us that all believers are the adopted children of God. It follows that each one is a full member of his family and household.

Paul is using picture after picture to explain great truths. The one which will dominate verses 20-22 is that of a building. To see it clearly, we must imagine two walls standing at right angles to each other. At first sight, it looks as if these two walls are nothing to do with each other. But they are, because they are both built on the same foundation (2:20). The Gentile wall and the Jewish wall are both built on the foundation of the apostles and prophets.

If you are a Christian at all, it is because you have come to believe the message proclaimed by those whom the Lord Jesus Christ appointed to be authoritative teachers and interpreters of the Christian faith — the apostles. The Spirit of Christ had already announced the same message in the Old Testament; it was he who was at work in each ancient prophet. There were also prophets in the New Testament church until such a time as the Scriptures were completed, and these received direct revelation from the same Christ, given by the same Spirit. All believers, whether their origin be Jewish or Gentile, build on the same foundation.

The two walls of which we are talking meet at a corner. Supporting that corner is the cornerstone. If that cornerstone were taken away, the whole structure would collapse. There is only one cornerstone for the two walls. It is the same for both. It is the Lord Jesus Christ. True faith, wherever it is found, relies entirely on him.

The picture continues in verses 21-22. The bricks which rest on this foundation and which rely entirely upon this cornerstone also fit into each other. They are **'joined together'** (2:21). Each believer is a brick and new bricks are being added all the time. The structure is thus seen to grow, and it is growing into a temple!

No Gentile believer has to stand outside and fondly long to be admitted into the temple. Together with other believers, whether they be Jew or Gentile, he or she *is* the temple! That is the only temple that God has today. In his providence, he swept the physical temple out of Jerusalem in A.D. 70 and it will never be rebuilt. Even if an earthly temple was rebuilt, God would have nothing to do with it. The only temple in which he is interested is that spiritual one which is composed of all believers put together. The true Israel and the true temple are one and the same thing. The new covenant is not about earthly nations and buildings. It is about the spiritual realities of which these things were only pictures.

The old temple was God's dwelling-place on earth. The new temple is his dwelling-place on earth. It is not in a physical structure anywhere, but in his spiritual temple, that the glory of God is seen in the world. No church, chapel, cathedral or basilica is graced with the presence of God. He lives in people, by his Spirit. There are no holy places on the whole of this planet. No believer needs them. He and all other Christians **'are being built together for a habitation of God in the Spirit'** (2:22).

What marvellous things God has done for us! He has given us all a memory, and commanded us never to forget what we once were. This we do with shame and horror. He also commands us never to forget what we now are. We do this with humility — we are only what we are because of the cross, but it was our sins that put his Son there. However, we also do it with rejoicing, for our privileges are greater than we could ever have imagined. We were once separated from God, but now we are united to him; what a wonder! We were once separated from each other; now we are one nation, not many; now we are one building, not just separate bricks, unconnected to each other.

Will we learn two important lessons from this section? The first is that we should glory in the cross. We should revel in it. What the Son of God has done for us by his death should be ever in our thoughts and constantly on our lips. Paul never tires of this theme, for he sees that all our privileges without exception depend on Calvary.

The second lesson concerns the unity of the church. We are not talking about that false unity which parades under the banner of the World Council of Churches and similar bodies which have no attachment to the gospel. We are talking about the unity of those who love and honour the Lord Jesus Christ, especially in the context of local churches. It makes a mockery of what we have seen in God's Word when individual bricks fall out with each other and behave as if they do not belong to each other. Next to God's law and the gospel itself, there is nothing more important on earth than the oneness and unity of those whom the Saviour has redeemed. If we do not believe that, we have not even begun to understand the passage we have just studied.

7.
Paul talks about himself

Please read Ephesians 3:1-13

In Ephesians 3:1-13 Paul talks about himself. Why does he do this? Writing as the apostle to the Gentiles, he has been telling new believers what has happened to them. Once they were spiritually dead, but now they are alive. Once they were both separated from God and his people, but now they are full members of Israel and are also the very temple in which God dwells.

Paul has been explaining to these believers what has happened to them because he had been praying that they might have understanding in this area. He is now on the point of telling them more about what he prays for them. As he opens chapter 3 it is his intention to tell them about this right away. By comparing 3:1 and 3:14 we can see that he planned to write, 'For this reason I, Paul, the prisoner of Jesus Christ for you Gentiles, bow my knees to the Father ...' But he never did so. As he dictated to his amanuensis, or secretary, the word 'Gentiles' triggered off a train of thought that he just had to pursue. He would come back to what he originally planned to say, but not immediately.

What was it about the word 'Gentiles' which temporarily diverted Paul? It is as if he said to himself: 'Gentiles? They are Gentiles and Christ appointed me to be the apostle to the Gentiles. Perhaps I had better tell them a little more about this. They need to know how this came to be, and what it means.' So Paul pursues this train of thought before returning to his main epistle. In doing so, he talks about himself, and gives us a glimpse of himself that we could not have in any other way. We see into his heart and character, and learn a great deal more about his message.

The passage before us is very rich and we are in danger of missing the wood for the trees. To prevent this happening we will deal with it simply, by asking two questions.

What sort of man was Paul?

1. A man with a strong view of providence (3:1)

The apostle opens this chapter with the following words: **'For this reason I, Paul, the prisoner of Jesus Christ for you Gentiles...'**
Everybody knew that Paul had a lot of time for the Gentiles. In fact, not so long ago, when he had been in Jerusalem, he had spent most of his time in the company of a Gentile, Trophimus, who was actually from Ephesus. The two were so constantly seen together that when Paul visited the temple, many people assumed that Paul must have taken this Gentile into the forbidden inner courts with him. This led to a riot, which in turn led to Paul being arrested. This was the beginning of a whole train of events which brought Paul as a prisoner to Rome, from where he was writing to the Ephesians. This explains how Paul could write that he was a 'prisoner ... for you Gentiles'.

But Paul did not write this in a bitter or resentful tone. He saw himself as 'the prisoner of Jesus Christ'. What did he mean by that? Why did he not say, rather, that he was the prisoner of the Romans? Although all that had happened to him was quite unfair, and what had taken place was genuinely distressing, Paul could see that an invisible hand was behind it all. Everything was happening 'according to the purpose of him who works all things after the counsel of his will' (1:11).

This understanding of events changed everything for the apostle. For him, the doctrine of God's sovereignty was not an abstract concept, but a truth to be lived by. He was in prison because the Lord Jesus Christ wanted it that way. He was therefore *his* prisoner. He would remain there as long as his Lord wanted, but not a moment longer. Meanwhile he would live to please him in the circumstances in which he had placed him. Humanly speaking it was very trying, and it certainly looked like a tragedy. But there are no accidents. Everything is part of a divine plan. It was a man who was inflexibly strong on that point who had first preached the gospel at Ephesus.

2. *A man with a clear sense of commission* (3:2,7)

Paul wonders if his Gentile readers **'have heard of the dispensation of the grace of God which was given to me for you'** (3:2). In fact, we can paraphrase him like this: 'I take it for granted that you have heard of me, and that you have heard that the grace of God not only saved me but put a gift in my hand. That gift which God's grace dispensed to me was not for me to enjoy selfishly. It was for you ...'

Paul has in mind the manager of a large estate putting differing responsibilities into the hands of various servants. The particular task given to him is to preach the gospel to the Gentiles. He is not self-appointed. This assignment has been entrusted to him by another. This he cannot forget. He is a man with a strong sense of commission.

Verse 7 brings this out with even greater force. Here he talks of the gospel **'of which I became a minister according to the gift of the grace of God given to me by the effective working of his power'**. Paul did not just wake up one day and think it was time to do something about the Gentiles. He did not make himself into a gospel minister. It was a function given to him by God's grace alone. And he who sent him to the work equipped him for it. He tells the Ephesians that he is energized by the mighty power of God in this service for the Lord. Of course, they themselves had seen his ministry in action. They were witnesses to how powerful it was. Many of them had been converted through it. How is it that a despised message preached by a weak and unimpressive orator had invincibly persuaded and conquered such a multitude? The apostle to the Gentiles was accompanied by the very power of the God who had sent him to the work.

3. *A man with an overwhelming sense of privilege* (3:8)

At the end of chapter 2 Paul told us never to forget what we once were. He himself had not. This is why he talks about himself as he does in verse 8: **'To me, who am less than the least of all the saints, this grace was given, that I should preach among the Gentiles the unsearchable riches of Christ.'**

He is just glad to be saved. He thinks of all those men and women that the Lord has set apart for himself — 'the saints', as the Bible calls them. He then thinks of the least and lowest among them. He sees himself as lower still. Had he not been a cruel and determined persecutor of the Lord's people? With blasphemies on his lips, had he not thrown many of them into prison? And now that he was one of their number, he scarcely felt he could lift up his head in their presence. What a privilege it was to belong to that company — a privilege of which he was not worthy! If a list were to be drawn up, with the greatest Christians at the top and the least at the bottom, he considered that his name would trail a long, long way below the lowest names.

This was the man whom Christ had called to preach! The Lord took the lowest name on the list and made him his special messenger to the Gentiles! What a responsibility and what a privilege! The appointment was not done on the basis of merit. It was all of grace.

And what could such a man preach? He could not blow his own trumpet, for there was nothing to make a noise about. He would preach what he was called to preach. He would stand up like a herald and proclaim Christ! We cannot even begin to imagine with what conviction Paul did that. He had shown Christ nothing but hatred; but Christ had shown him nothing but love. His love was without bounds. His person was beyond description. His work was eternal in both its plan and effect. His ways were beyond finding out. He could never tell all, but he would tell all that he could. He would preach among the Gentiles the unfathomable, the unsearchable riches of Christ!

4. A man more concerned with others than with himself (3:1-2,13)

This comes across in the opening words of the chapter. Paul knows that he would not be in prison at all if it were not for the Gentiles (3:1), but there is no trace of irritation as he mentions it. He has no thought for himself. Nor does he in verse 2, where he talks of his commission to the ministry. Years after receiving that commision, he still speaks of the ministry in an unselfish way. There was nothing in it for him. He exercised it for the benefit of others.

It is, however, verse 13 which is unusually striking: **'I ask that you do not lose heart at my tribulations for you, which is your glory.'** He has only one thought in his mind and it does not concern himself. He is praying that the Ephesians and other Gentile believers might not be disheartened by what he is going through! The fact that he is suffering himself is not something he pauses to think about. But he is worried about the effect that his imprisonment might be having on others.

To encourage his readers, Paul tells them that his time in prison is their 'glory'. He was not there because he had something to be ashamed of. He was suffering because he had freely preached the gospel to the Gentiles. He was there for a worthwhile cause and they ought to be proud of the fact. They should be speaking positively about it. The apostle to the Gentiles was suffering because he taught that Gentiles who came to Christ were as much God's people as any Jewish believer, ancient or modern.

Unselfishness is a very rare commodity. We now understand why Paul did not spare himself in any way when he first proclaimed Christ at Ephesus. He tells us about that himself in Acts 20:17-38. His one concern was to bring blessings to others, whatever the cost in personal terms. Years later, in his Roman prison, he was no different. Nor did he think only of the Ephesians at that time, but of the Philippians, the Colossians and Philemon, to whom he also wrote letters. Spiritual work can be done only by people who put themselves out.

5. A man enjoying fellowship with God (3:12)

To find out about this we must go to verse 12. What Paul says here is rendered more powerful by the fact that his fellowship with God is more hinted at than stated.

Referring to our Lord Jesus Christ, Paul talks of him as the one **'in whom we have boldness and access with confidence through faith in him'**. As he speaks about Christ, Paul immediately thinks of him as the one by whom we may come boldly to God's throne. The mere mention of his name sets Paul thinking about going to God as confidently as a child skips to his father. The terror of approaching him has gone. We have access into the holiest. It is a privilege which becomes ours through faith.

The prisoner's mind ran naturally along these lines. There can be only one explanation for this: in that Roman cell he himself was enjoying such fellowship with God. The prison walls were impregnated with the spirit of prayer. They provided no obstacle to prayer. There, where fear usually reigned, a man was being bold. There, where doors were closed and bolted, he was enjoying access. Where others were losing confidence, he was enjoying it. With the eyes of faith he was looking away from himself, towards his Mediator, the Lord Jesus Christ. There, where no earthly circumstance was favourable, he was having communion with the King of heaven, the living and true God.

What sort of message did he preach?

We have seen a little of Paul the man. Very few men like him have ever walked across the stage of history. Was his message equally unusual? What sort of message was it?

1. A revealed message (3:3-5)

Paul states that **'By revelation [God] made known to me the mystery (as I wrote before in a few words, by which, when you read, you may understand my knowledge in the mystery of Christ), which in other ages was not made known to the sons of men, as it has now been revealed by the Spirit to his holy apostles and prophets'** (3:3-5).

There was nothing manmade about the apostle's message. God himself had revealed it to him. Not only so, but God had given him an inspired understanding of it, as should have been clear to the Ephesians from things he had previously written to them. No revelation as clear as this had ever been given before. But the Holy Spirit had now given it to the apostles whom the Lord had set aside — of whom Paul was one — and also to other people who were receiving direct revelation at that time, namely the prophets who were found in the early church until the time that the Scriptures had been completed.

No one is receiving direct revelation today. But this does not mean that the message which Paul is speaking about is lost. It is contained in those writings of the apostles and their associates which the Holy Spirit has seen fit to preserve, one of which we are studying at this very moment.

2. A mystery (3:3-7)

In verses 3-7 Paul twice describes his message as a 'mystery' (3:3,4). Today we use this word to speak of an unexplained riddle, such as 'the mystery of the *Marie Céleste*', the sailing ship found in perfect shape on the high seas, but with nobody on board. But we must never think that the Bible uses words in exactly the same way as we do. Paul's message was not an unexplained riddle to which only he and a few others had the solution.

The word 'mystery' in God's Word refers to something which has been hidden, but which is now revealed. Something previously concealed is now open to view. What was covered is now unveiled. The emphasis is not so much that something had been kept secret, but that it has now been made known.

'The mystery' mentioned here is a truth which had never been understood before. It had been kept hidden. Then it was revealed to someone as unlikely as the persecutor converted on the Damascus road, as well as to the other apostles and the New Testament prophets.

And what *was* that mystery? The Old Testament had revealed that the number of believing Jews would get less and less until there was only a remnant left. It had also revealed that great numbers of Gentiles were going to enter God's salvation. All this was plain. But it was never revealed that the believing Jews and the believing Gentiles were going to become one body. It was never disclosed that the believing Gentiles would be on the same footing as their Jewish counterparts, and that they would become one spiritual nation. Nobody in the Old Testament envisaged that the coming of God's Messiah would one day totally remove the barrier between Jews and Gentiles who came to him, and that it would not matter a scrap whether you were one or the other.

The Gentiles were going to be **'fellow heirs'** (3:6) and not in any way restricted to second-rate blessings! They were going to be **'of the same body'** (3:6), full members of Israel, and not in any sense outside it. They were going to be **'partakers of [God's] promise in Christ through the gospel'** (3:6). They would share just as much in the covenant promises as any native-born Hebrew! Every individual believer, whether his or her origin was Jewish or Gentile, was going to have exactly the same status!

This was 'the mystery'. The first to see it were the apostles and the New Testament prophets (3:5). One of those apostles was Paul who, being the apostle to the Gentiles, had a fuller understanding of it than the others, and preached it with directness and power (3:4,7). His writings have been with us now for nearly 2,000 years. But the

majority of believers have still not really grasped what he has to say.
The idea is still widespread that the Jews have privileges into which
the Gentiles cannot enter. There are still Christians who believe that
the unfulfilled prophecies of the Old Testament refer to the Jews,
whereas in fact they speak about the whole people of God. Many
believers consider that the Old Testament is not really much to do
with them, forgetting that every one of God's people is a beneficiary
of its covenants and authorized to enjoy its promises. They have
never grasped the mystery.

God has only one people, not two. There are two sorts of people
in the world, it is true, but they are the lost and the saved. The saved
are not sub-divided into two categories. They form just one body.
They make up only one building. Christ's blood has as surely
washed away their divisions as it has their sins.

3. A message for the world (3:8-9)

Paul writes, **'To me, who am less than the least of all the saints,
this grace was given, that I should preach among the Gentiles
the unsearchable riches of Christ, and to make all people see
what is the fellowship of the mystery, which from the beginning
of the ages has been hidden in God who created all things
through Jesus Christ'** (3:8-9).

Paul's commission and desire were to proclaim everything that
there was to say about Christ. Christ himself was sending him to
preach to the Gentiles. Everybody was to know about the mystery.
Its hiding place had been in God himself — God the Creator of the
whole world, and all worlds. Having now revealed the mystery,
God's will was that the whole world should hear about it. He made
the world through Jesus Christ, and the mystery is about Jesus Christ
and about how those who are divided may have perfect fellowship
with each other through him.

Where men and women are right with God through Christ, they
are right with each other, whatever may have divided them before.
Unconverted people in the world may learn to co-exist peacefully,
or even to enjoy each other's company. But they know nothing of
fellowship. Fellowship exists where all people stand on the same
footing and enjoy the same rights, privileges and responsibilities. It
is not just that their distinctions are tolerated, or put aside. They do
not even exist! And so it is when we are in Christ. How this sad world
needs such a message as this!

4. *A message for the angels* (3:10)

Paul has been sent to preach the mystery to the world **'to the intent that now the manifold wisdom of God might be made known by the church to the principalities and powers in the heavenly places'** (3:10).

Observing and scrutinizing what goes on in this world are great numbers of angels, both good and bad. One of the reasons that God sends out his gospel, with its revelation of 'the mystery', is to teach *them* something! By looking at the Christian church on earth, these 'principalities and powers in the heavenly places' actually come to a fuller appreciation of 'the manifold wisdom of God'.

The Greek word translated 'manifold' is a very difficult word to put into English. Some writers have used the word 'many-splendoured' to convey its meaning to us. One diamond can be breathtaking in its beauty. It can sparkle with a thousand colours as its many facets reflect and refract a single light. But a diamond is nothing compared with the wisdom of God. It has so many facets that not even the angels have seen them all. They have not even seen all the colours that come from just one side.

Both the holy and fallen angels know that the infinitely wise God is going to bring about his eternal purpose of saving a people for his Son. As they look over the earth, they see the church. In that church they see both Jewish and Gentile believers, redeemed in exactly the same way, called by one gospel and enjoying identical privileges. These angels have been surveying the world since human history began, but nothing like this existed before Calvary. And there is nothing like it anywhere else in the universe. And so the gospel message brings them to see facets of God's wisdom which they did not even imagine existed.

5. *A message bringing to pass an eternal purpose* (3:11)

The calling of Paul as a preacher, the propagation of 'the mystery' and its effect upon the angels are all **'according to the eternal purpose which [God] accomplished in Christ Jesus our Lord'** (3:11).

God has a plan, and that plan is as eternal as he is. We learned a good deal about this in chapter 1, and other parts of the Bible have a lot to say about it as well. God's eternal Son, our Lord Jesus Christ, is at the centre of the plan and it will come to pass through him. So certain is the fulfilment of God's purpose that Paul can talk about it as being already accomplished.

God's plan is to bring home to the eternal fold all his sheep. He gave them to the Lord Jesus Christ before the world began, and it is that Good Shepherd who died for them. They come to follow the Shepherd when they hear his voice, and that voice is heard through the faithful announcement of the gospel. This last point is particularly important and we drew attention to it when we studied 2:7. Widely differing sheep all hear the same voice, and so there comes to be 'one flock and one shepherd' (John 10:16) — which is precisely 'the mystery' about which Paul has said so much.

The preaching of the gospel is said to be according to God's eternal purpose (3:11) because that purpose was not going to be brought about without such preaching. It is an integral part of the plan. It is an essential link in the chain, forged on the same anvil and by the same Blacksmith as all the other links. Paul could not forget this. Every time he got up to preach he had this in mind. His preaching was actually bringing to pass, in time and space, the eternal purpose of God! No wonder he felt unworthy to preach. No wonder he discharged his commission with such faithfulness, courage and perseverance. No wonder he spoke with such authority. The words he spoke were of eternal significance!

Paul has spoken about himself. But he has not drawn attention to himself. He is the man he is because of Christ. He would have neither message nor ministry, were it not for Christ. Christ is the source of all that Paul has. He knows one who gives and gives but never becomes poorer. His riches are without limit. Paul has spoken about himself that we might admire Christ!

8.
Renewed prayer

Please read Ephesians 3:14-21

We come now to one of the most sublime passages of the New Testament. In chapter 1, Paul assured the new believers at Ephesus that he was praying for them. He told them that he was praying that they might understand where they were going, and what had happened to them. But that was not the sum total of his intercession. Here in 3:14-21, he discloses what else he was praying for on behalf of the Christians of the first-century pagan city.

This is a passage of indescribable grandeur. There is a magnificence about it which raises us to the heights. And yet the casket which contains such jewels is plain and unadorned. The passage divides quite simply into three parts.

Paul's approach (3:14-15)

Paul begins this section with the words: **'For this reason...'** (3:14). He is taking up what he was originally going to write in 3:1, where the same words occur. To find out, therefore, what the 'reason' for his prayer is, we must go back to the teaching immediately preceding 3:1. There he was telling us that there are no longer Jews and Gentiles in God's sight. Jews who believe, together with Gentiles who believe, all form just one nation; they make up a single spiritual temple. This is 'the mystery' of which he has just been speaking in his parenthesis of 3:1-13. All believers, whatever their background, enjoy identical privileges.

As Paul thinks about this, it moves him to pray for the Ephesian believers. After all, everything he was saying could be seen in their own experience. Jews and Gentiles, rich and poor, slaves and free had become one body, and constituted one local church at Ephesus. 'The mystery' was taking visible form on Ephesian soil. Paul sees it, and goes to his knees to ask God to grant further favours to these people.

How does he approach God? **'I bow my knees to the Father of our Lord Jesus Christ,'** he says (3:14). Knees bent, he does homage to God. He approaches God as King. He is the great God of whom the apostle has spoken so highly many times in this letter. Prostrate and in utter abasement, he must come as a suppliant before the throne.

But he also approaches God as Father. He bows his knees **'to the Father of our Lord Jesus Christ, from whom the whole family in heaven and earth is named'** (3:14-15). God has one eternally begotten Son, the Lord Jesus Christ. He also has an immense number of adopted sons. Each one has been named with his name. Some of these adopted children are now with the Father in heaven, while others are at this moment living on the earth. But whether they are in heaven or on earth, they form a single family, and there is only one Father.

Generally speaking, Christians tend to fall into one of two extremes when they pray. There are those who see only the greatness and majesty of God and who speak to him as if he were distant and almost unknowable. There are others who seem only to remember that he is our Father and who often address him with sickening intimacy. Paul avoids both these dangers. He is exactly in line with the teaching of our Lord Jesus Christ who told us to pray to God as our Father, but all the time to remember that he is the one who is in heaven, whose name is to be hallowed.

I shall never forget once sitting at supper with a minister and his wife and a theological lecturer who, like me, was a visitor to their home. The lady of the house was dressed up to the nines and spent the evening tut-tutting about the young people of their church. They were coming to the services dressed in jeans, and more and more of the young men were coming without a tie. They wouldn't dress like that if they were going to see the queen! Didn't they have any respect? Didn't they realize that the God they came to worship was the King of Kings?

I looked across at the theological lecturer. He had a tie but it was loose, and the top of his shirt was undone. His coloured trousers attracted my eye, which then spotted his trendy shoes. He smiled as his gentle question interrupted the elegant tirade: 'Yes, God is our King; but is he not also our Father?'

How we dress in church is entirely a matter of Christian liberty. But we have no liberty in choosing how to pray. If we do not bow in heartfelt reverence before the King, our prayer life is defective. But we are the King's sons! Princes may speak to their father with an openness which mere courtiers would never dare to use.

Paul's petitions (3:16-19)

We have seen how Paul approached God. Both these aspects come out once more in the actual requests that he makes. He believes that God is well able to grant them because of **'the riches of his glory'** (3:16). Paul sees him as a majestic King of obvious wealth. Then in verse 19 he uses the expression: **'that you may be filled with all the fulness of God'**. I personally would prefer to translate that in this way: 'that you might be filled unto all the fulness of God'. Let me explain.

Imagine being invited to a restaurant by the wealthiest man in the land. What would you choose from the menu? Certainly not egg and chips! You would not mind running up quite a heavy bill, knowing that your host's wallet would stretch to that without effort. You could ask and ask, up to the limit of his ability to give.

There is no limit to God's giving because he, by definition, is limitless. So Paul says, 'I am requesting that you might experience certain things unto the fulness of God. I am asking that you might be filled and filled up to the limit of God's ability to give. But there is no limit! So I am praying that you might be filled unto all the fulness of God.'

Paul sees God as a King. And as he prays he expects to be heard. He expects that the slaves and the children of the Ephesian church, as well as all the others, will receive what he prays for. Now why should God bother with slaves? Why should he bother with any of the Christians at Ephesus? Why should he listen to Paul's prayer at all? Simply because he is the Father of his people. God can be confidently addressed as King. He can be boldly addressed as Father. That is why Paul comes to him with his requests.

And what are those requests? There are three of them and each one begins with the word 'that': 'For this reason I bow my knees ... *that* he would grant you, according to the riches of his glory, to be strengthened with might through his Spirit in the inner man, *that* Christ may dwell in your hearts through faith; *that* you, being rooted and grounded in love, may be able to comprehend with all the saints what is the width and length and depth and height — to know the love of Christ which passes knowledge; that you may be filled with all the fulness of God' (3:16-17).

Paul is praying concerning their wills, their hearts and their minds. In his prayer he speaks about the Father, the Son and the Holy Spirit. He is praying that the whole of the Godhead will do something for the whole man. His prayer does not mention externals, for the gospel is not concerned with them. He is praying for something to happen inside the lives of the Ephesians.

1. To do with the will   (3:16)

Mary is a Christian who works as a typist in an office where there are no other believers. She spends each working day without any Christian fellowship. For all practical purposes she is also separated from her Bible. She can read it at home as the day starts, but once at work there is no further opportunity.

In the office is a pleasant young man who repeatedly asks Mary to go out with him. She knows that a Christian may never court a non-Christian. It is an offence against God. But this young man's insistence and charm are too much for her. Eventually she does what she knows to be wrong. Why is that? It is because she is not strong enough spiritually. She needs inward might.

John is a believer from the same church, but his problem is different. In his factory everyone has forty-five minutes for lunch. When the time is up nobody is ready to restart. They are still drinking their tea or doing their crosswords. John knows that he should get up and go back to his machine, but he does not like to do it. The others will think that he is pointing the finger at them, or that he is a 'creep' trying to impress the management. So John sits still and says nothing. He gives in to the silent group pressure and, each day, steals ten or fifteen minutes of his boss's time. How weak he is! He needs inward might.

But not every believer is like these two. Many of them have a certain strength about them, an inward resolve and determination. They are gracious but principled. Even mockery cannot move them from doing what they know to be right. They were not like this when they were unconverted. It is obviously a work of the Spirit which has made them into the people they now are. Paul prays that God, according to the riches of his glory, would grant each Ephesian believer **'to be strengthened with might through his Spirit in the inner man'** (3:16). It is much better to pray for young Christians than to criticize them.

2. To do with the heart (3:17)

'I am also praying,' says Paul, **'that Christ may dwell in your hearts through faith'**, or 'that Christ may be at home in your hearts, by faith', as many Greek scholars have interpreted it.

We shall understand this if we take the time to read John 14:15-24. Would you be willing to do that before going any further? It is a passage in which the Lord Jesus Christ explains that those who love him keep his commandments. Those who do not keep his commandments have no real love for him at all.

The passage contains some startling promises. Jesus says that if we do what he says, he will manifest himself in our lives (John 14:21). He will be a living reality to us. By means of the Helper, the Holy Spirit, he will make himself at home in our hearts. We shall have the consciousness, not only that he is *with* us, but that he is *in* us (John 14:17). 'If anyone loves me, he will keep my word; and my Father will love him, and we will come to him and *make our home* with him' (John 14:23, italics mine).

That is what Paul is talking about here. When a person puts God's Word into practice, he has a sense of Christ's presence in his life. But why should anyone obey God's Word? Because he *believes* it. Christ's being 'at home' in our hearts is linked to faith.

If Mary and John had known inward spiritual strength, they would not have been so weak. They would have obeyed God's Word and enjoyed this unveiling of Christ in their lives of which we are speaking. His presence *in* them would have been more real to them than the presence of those around them. They would have walked with him, and therefore would not have walked as they did. Paul prayed for all the Marys and Johns of Ephesus. Who is praying for those who live today?

3. To do with the mind (3:17-19)

Paul's third request is to do with the mind. He is praying that his
readers, inwardly strengthened by God's Spirit and filled with love
for Christ, will be able to comprehend something which is beyond
comprehension, to know something which is unknowable! (3:17-
19).

Whatever does he mean? We shall understand it well enough if
we think of a group of researchers who are sent to explore an ocean.
They must find out how wide it is, and how long and how deep.
When their research is over, all of them know something about the
ocean. Each one knows something that nobody else knows. Each
person is in a position to tell all the rest something he has discovered.
And yet there is not one of them who knows everything that there is
to be known. Nor do all of them put together. And yet every explorer
knows something of the greatness of that ocean.

'I am praying that you might see Christ's love like this,' says
Paul, knowing full well that no one can ever discover its full
dimensions. He wants us to explore its width. There is a marvellous
breadth about it. It embraces not only the Jew, but the Gentile as
well. There is a wide invitation to come to Christ. Not even all the
church put together has yet realized how wide the love of Christ
really is.

And what is the length of Christ's love? It is from eternity to
eternity. He loved us before the world began, he loves us now, and
he will still be loving us a million million years after it has ended.
Who can measure that?

Who knows how deep Christ's love is? It was his love which
brought him to descend from heaven. It was love which moved him
to sit with sinners, even with those who had sunk to the very depths.
Paul knew more about those depths than most. Very few people have
been deeper than he went; yet Christ's love met him there.

Can anyone explain how high Christ's love is? Think of the
height to which he has already lifted us. We are the adopted children
of God, already seated in heavenly places. We know we are going
to enter into our inheritance, but still 'It has not yet been revealed
what we shall be' (1 John 3:2). We are going to be lifted to heights
of glory which the Bible has not even begun to describe!

Who, then, knows **'what is the width and length and depth
and height'**? (3:18). We all know something about it. Some know
more about the width than the depth. Others know more about the

length than the height. We all know more about Christ's love than we used to. However, if all believers of all times were to tell what they knew, we should still not discover the whole. 'But I am praying', says the apostle, 'that you and all saints will explore the love of Christ, and have limitless experiences of it unto all the fulness of God.'

No Christian has gone as far as it is possible to go. No believer has yet understood all that there is to understand. There are limitless panoramas just waiting to be seen and enjoyed. There are endless dimensions of spiritual experience to be entered into. No number can be put on the discoveries that have yet to be made. Who would be foolish enough to be content with his present level of spiritual understanding and enjoyment? Shall we not give all our energy to making spiritual progress? And shall we not pray for each other as Paul prayed for the Ephesians?

Paul's doxology (3:20-21)

These things being so, Paul has to turn from his prayer for his readers as his enraptured soul erupts in praise to God. Standing on the shore of the ocean his spiritual eye glimpses four things.

1. An attribute (3:20)

'Now to him who is able to do exceedingly abundantly above all that we ask or think, according to the power that works in us...' he begins (3:20). Paul reflects on the fact that there is no limit to what God can do for us. No limit! He is able to do what we ask; all that we ask; above all that we ask; abundantly above all that we ask; exceedingly abundantly above all that we ask; exceedingly abundantly above all that we ask or think!

Have you ever limited God? Have you sat down and said inside you, 'There's nothing more he can do for me'? Away with such thoughts! Look what he is able to do! See the attribute and join in the doxology.

2. A desire (3:21)

'To him be glory', Paul continues. Oh, how he desires that the Ephesians might receive and experience all that he has prayed for them. But there is something he wants much more than that. He wants God to be glorified. He wants him to be worshipped, exalted and adored. He wants him to receive all credit, and for all creatures everywhere to think high thoughts about him. Is there anyone who has read these first three chapters of Ephesians who does not have a similar desire?

3. A place (3:21)

'To him be glory in the church by Christ Jesus,' cries the worshipping apostle. Whoever else will or not will not praise God, the church must do it. And what is 'the church'? It is that company of people who approach God solely on the basis of what he has done for them through the Lord Jesus Christ. They come to God by him. And what is the first and highest task of the church? It is not primarily to be a fellowship or to evangelize, though these responsibilities are truly important. It is to prostrate itself before its God and to glorify him!

4. A time (3:21)

'To him be glory in the church by Christ Jesus throughout all ages, world without end. Amen.' Paul desires that this omnipotent God should be glorified in the church for ever and ever and ever. The praise begun on earth is to continue into the world to come, and is never to end. 'So be it!' concludes the apostle. And how could he wish for anything less? Infinite love deserves infinite praise. Such praise can only be given in an eternal world. But we can begin our doxologies before we get there.

9.
The unity of the church

Please read Ephesians 4:1-16

The first three chapters of Ephesians are now behind us. They were doctrinal: they were mostly about what we are to believe. We now come to the practical chapters. Because a Christian believes in a certain way, he or she is to behave in a certain way. Paul is going to build on the foundation he has laid and tell us how to live the Christian life — at church, in the world and at home. He will then remind us of our spiritual warfare before bringing his letter to a close.

The easiest place to live the Christian life is at church, and this is where Paul starts his practical instruction. His particular theme is the unity of the church. In his mind, of course, is the church at Ephesus, but his teaching applies to any local assembly of Christians.

We will remember that Paul has been showing us that the old distinctions are now finished in God's sight. There are no longer Jews and Gentiles and it is a mistake to resurrect these differences. God does not have two peoples, but one. There are no longer two sorts of walls in the building; both are built on the same foundation, meet at the same cornerstone and fit into each other. 'The mystery' takes on visible form in the local church. It would therefore be both wrong and tragic for there to be disunity there.

We are reading Ephesians almost two thousand years after it was written, but its teachings are as relevant as ever. Many local churches are riddled with tensions and suspicion. They are troubled with cliques and splinter groups. Some of them split and then split again. Those who think they are immune to such difficulties often prove to be most susceptible to them. With deep pastoral concern, Paul addresses this issue in 4:1-16. He has four telling points to make. His teaching is needed by us all.

Unity is not automatic (4:1-3)

If it were, this paragraph would not have needed to be written! Unity is not something that just happens; it has to be worked for. In verse 1 Paul reminds his readers that he is in prison. He has already told them that he is there for their sake. He does not pull rank on them and say, 'Look, I'm the apostle to the Gentiles, so you must do as I say.' Nor does he flatter them. His words are: **'I, therefore, the prisoner of the Lord, beseech you to lead a life worthy of the calling with which you were called'** (4:1).

From his prison cell he pleads with the men and women of a local church to remember that they have been called by God and that a certain sort of behaviour is therefore expected of them. They are no longer like others, so they can no longer live like others. Called out of the world by God to be his people, they must live in a way which is consistent with this fact.

Unity in the local church depends upon each person in it cultivating certain attitudes. They are **'lowliness and gentleness, with long-suffering, bearing with one another in love'** (4:2). Lowliness is taking the lowest place with a view to being the servant of all. The Lord Jesus Christ was lowly, and so was Paul, as we saw in 3:8. Disunity cannot survive where lowliness reigns.

With lowliness is to go 'gentleness', or 'meekness', as older translations put it. It means being spiritually and morally strong without being self-assertive, pushy or heavy-handed. Its strength is controlled.

'Long-suffering' is being hurt and hurt again, but not complaining, while those who are 'bearing with another in love' are refusing to strike back or be bitter. Such people do not consider that their own feelings matter. What counts is the welfare of others. All the qualities mentioned in these verses are found in our Lord Jesus Christ himself, and his church is to be modelled on him.

Those who are aiming to have such Christlike lives may truly be said to be **'endeavouring to keep the unity of the Spirit in the bond of peace'** (4:3). You have to work to maintain unity, but nobody has to create it. It exists already. All divisive barriers have been removed by the work of Christ. The members of the new nation and family are bound both to God and to each other. The Spirit-forged bonds exist. But they have to be preserved.

Sadly, many believers make no effort in this area, which is why Paul is writing about it. War is waged where Christ has made peace. The God-given bonds are forgotten. Ungodly attitudes, words and actions raise the old divisions again. Many such people believe Ephesians chapters 1-3 in theory, but openly contradict it in practice. God's sanctifying call is forgotten and the redeemed church disgraces itself by resembling the perishing world.

Paul pleads for different behaviour. He calls for the execution of self and all else that smacks of 'me first'. Unity is not automatic. Steps must be taken to preserve it. Work is needed. Who will make the necessary effort?

Unity is logical (4:4-6)

Do you sometimes look at other Christians and wonder how much you really have in common with them? We are such an assorted bunch! We come from different backgrounds and nations; we vary in intellect, achievement, social status and wealth; we represent a whole spectrum of characters, hang-ups and eccentricities, and express widely contrasting likes and dislikes! There are so many differences between us. What really do we have in common?

All the distinctions we have mentioned are temporary. But there are seven eternal realities which we possess in common with all believers everywhere. What we share is immeasurably greater than what differentiates us. It is not logical that we should live in any form of disunity.

What are these seven eternal realities? They are spelled out for us in verses 4-6: **'There is one body and one Spirit, just as you were called in one hope of your calling; one Lord, one faith, one baptism; one God and Father of all, who is above all, and through all, and in you all.'**

There is *one body*. Each local church is a microcosm, or miniature representation, of the whole church. And the church is a body. Its head is the Lord Jesus Christ, and each member is an organ, such as an ear, an eye or a foot. Those organs are members of one another.

They belong to each other and depend on each other. What folly it would be to chop the body up into separate pieces! How illogical and stupid it would be to set eye against ear, and foot against hand! Only unity is logical.

There is *one Spirit*. If you believe the gospel at all, it is because the Spirit has opened your understanding to see the truth of it. And if anyone else believes, the explanation is the same. There are not several spirits bringing people from unbelief to Christ. We are all animated by the one Spirit of God, and he it is who gives us the family-feeling we have towards fellow-Christians. Only unity is logical.

There is *one calling*, 'just as you were called in one hope of your calling' (4:4). Paul has already talked about the hope God's calling gives us in 1:18. The same God calls us to the same privileges and the same destination. We cannot behave as if we were on different roads bound for different places. Only unity is logical.

There is *one Lord*. That Lord is Jesus Christ. All who believe were chosen in him. They were redeemed by him. They follow him. It is under his lordship, and his alone, that they live. They are going to be with him. On what basis, then, can they think of disowning each other? Only unity is logical.

There is *one faith*. We have heard the same truths, we believe the same truths, and we rely upon the same truths for our eternal salvation. The people who believe the gospel are very diverse indeed, but there is still only one gospel. Saving faith is found in widely differing hearts, but that faith is the same in them all. We came to faith from different starting-points, but the faith we arrived at is identical. True faith does not scatter people. It joins them together. Only unity is logical.

There is *one baptism*. Baptism in the Holy Spirit is what inaugurates you into the spiritual dimension and makes you a member of Christ's body (1 Cor. 12:13). That is the spiritual reality. Baptism in water is not something different. It is the outward and visible sign of what has happened to you inwardly and invisibly. You receive it when you formally and publicly associate yourself with the body of which, spiritually, you are already a member. So the two baptisms are one. Every believer has received the spiritual reality, and in New Testament days every believer had also received the physical sign — wherever they had come from, and however great their human differences. How can people who have all declared their death to self and their allegiance to the Father, the Son and the Holy Spirit — how can these people then live as if they were members of warring clans? Only unity is logical.

There is *one God and Father of all,* 'who is above all, and through all, and in you all' (4:6). We gather round the same throne and whisper the sweet name of 'Father' to the one who sits there. He is our King and 'above' us all. We are his temple, as we learned in chapter 2, so he is 'through' us all. The heart of each individual believer is his shrine, so by his Spirit he is 'in' us all. In the light of all this, how can we keep apart from each other? How can we behave as if we belonged more to some of his children than others? To split from other believers is to say that all these truths are lies. But they are not! Only unity is logical.

Unity is not uniformity (4:7-12)

The fact that we are all *one* does not mean that we are all the *same*! There is no uniform for Christians to wear. It would be wrong if there were. We are all very different and God wants it that way. We have already spoken at length about our differences of background, culture, education and temperament. These distinctions exist but, for the reasons we have seen, they are not to affect the unity of the church. Unity there is; uniformity there never will be.

But there are differences between us in an area which we have not spoken about yet. It is in the sphere of spiritual gifts. Without exception, every one of us has received a gracious gift from Christ (4:7). The gifts are different, as we shall see, but the source of them all is the same.

What is Paul saying to us in verses 8-10? The main points are that Christ distributes spiritual gifts according to his own will, and that the giving of them flows from his ascension.

As Paul considers Christ's bodily return to heaven, which he sees referred to in Psalm 68:18, he thinks of a well-known practice of his time. If Roman generals were immensely successful in war, a great parade was organized for them on their return to the capital. Trailing in the triumphal procession would be numbers of captives taken by that general in his engagements with the enemy. He would lead captivity captive. The general would then sit on an elevated chair and give out the plunder seized in war. This would go to those who had fought with him and for him. Very different gifts would go to very differing people.

Paul has to adapt this illustration when he talks of our Lord Jesus Christ. He has won an immense victory by his death and resurrection. In triumph he has **'ascended far above all the heavens, that he might fill all things'** (4:10). There is nowhere that Christ does not reign — he who came to the very lowest place of all!

There are captives in Christ's great triumphal procession. *We* are those captives and we are taken, not in chains, but to sit in heavenly places with him. It is to those same captives that the Conqueror dispenses his widely varying gifts. Oh, the grace of God!

To illustrate what an array of different gifts there are, Paul talks about one aspect only of Christian work — the founding of a local church. He is, after all, writing to local church members about their life as a church. What he says is also a short summary of how the church at Ephesus itself came into being.

Verses 11-12 give his teaching. First of all the ascended Christ sends into an area an apostle. An apostle is an authoritative teacher and interpreter of the Christian faith, appointed to this task by the risen Christ whom he has seen physically. Paul was such an apostle and he was the first person to bring the gospel to Ephesus. There are no apostles today, but this fact does not spoil what the apostle is saying. His point is that Christ gives differing gifts to people in order to meet differing needs. As it happens, Christ still raises up men who have the gift of announcing his gospel in pioneer situations.

After apostles come prophets. These are people who receive new revelation directly from God and faithfully transmit it to the church. It was very important that there should be prophets in the New Testament churches. For many decades those churches had no Scriptures except the Old Testament. Many truths which the Christian church needs are not found in the Old Testament — such as 'the mystery' which Paul spoke about in chapter 3. These truths were revealed to the New Testament prophets until such a time as God's written revelation was complete. After that there was no need for this particular spiritual gift and it has disappeared. But this does not detract from what Paul is saying. Apostles and prophets exercise very different gifts! Yet it is Christ who sends them both, for both are necessary.

After prophets come evangelists. 'Evangel' means 'gospel', so we could translate 'evangelist' as 'gospeller'. As soon as local churches are founded, false teachers try to infiltrate them. These people have all the right vocabulary but they use it in a different sense. New Christians are easily taken in by them and very soon believe a 'gospel' which is not the true gospel at all, but only someone's invented version of it. So 'gospellers' are needed to keep on defining the true gospel in the face of subtle enemies who would destroy it. Timothy was such an evangelist and Paul sent him to ward off false teachers in Ephesus, as well as in other churches he had founded. We read about this in 1 and 2 Timothy, and especially in 2 Timothy 4:5. Titus was another. Paul's epistle to him reveals how he had sent him to resist false teachers who had come to Crete.

Apostles, prophets, evangelists; how different were their gifts! All were sent by the ascended Christ. All were working for the church's good. They worked harmoniously together without being squeezed into the same mould. Unity does not imply uniformity.

No church has ever needed these three gifts for ever. But there is a spiritual gift which no local church can do without. There must be **'pastors and teachers'** — the expression speaks of one function, not two. But what precisely are these people?

The word 'pastor' means 'shepherd'. Christ sends certain men to be his under-shepherds. Their responsibility is to tend his sheep. Their supreme task is to lead them into good pasture and to nourish them, all the time protecting them from what might harm them. How are spiritual sheep fed? By the Word of God, of course. This explains why 'pastors and teachers' are one and the same people.

But 'pastors and teachers' are not sent that God's people might remain passive. Christ has sent them **'for the equipping of the saints for the work of ministry, for the edifying of the body of Christ'** (4:12). As these men teach, those who listen to them realize that they themselves have a task to perform. The teaching they receive equips them spiritually. In this way each member of the church sets off to do his particular work. The gifts which are exercised are extremely diverse, but everyone works 'for the profit of all' (1 Cor. 12:7). In this way the whole body is edified, or built up. Unity is maintained but diversity is not destroyed.

We simply must not expect everybody to be the same! Our different abilities and opportunities have been given by Christ himself. Nobody must flatter himself and nobody must be jealous of anybody else. We can all do something to help build up the body. As we listen to our pastors and teachers expounding the Word, we shall find our hearts being stirred to do this or that in the cause of Christ. By doing those things we shall discover that the Lord has given us other talents that we knew nothing about. As we exercise those as well, the church will be even richer, and so shall we. The unity of the church and the diversity of its members will become more and more evident, and we shall be unable to hold back our admiration for the Head who has arranged things this way.

Unity is married to maturity (4:13-16)

We have just been talking about every member living for the welfare of the body and what happens as a result. Something else that happens is that the body comes to a common understanding of the faith. This is explained in verse 13. The different spiritual gifts do not divide the body, but unite it. Each one of them contributes something to the body's knowledge of the Son of God. And so the church grows spiritually. It leaves behind childhood and presses forward towards maturity. The image on which it is modelling itself, and into which it is being shaped, is that of the Lord Jesus Christ himself. The church never loses sight of this ideal, works constantly towards it and feels it cannot be satisfied with anything less than perfection, **'the measure of the stature of the fulness of Christ'** (4:13).

Oh, how Paul desires that the Ephesians **'should no longer be children'**! (4:14). With immaturity goes gullibility. Infants are easily taken in or tricked and, sadly, there are too many wicked people waiting to prey on them. If they were more mature they would not be so easily deceived. Paul has in mind the false teachers of whom we were speaking a little earlier. Infantile minds believe whatever is said to them. Their opinions are decided by the external influences which surround them. Blown about in all directions, they have no settled convictions of their own. Wherever there is restlessness there is discord. There can be no unity where there is not a common mind. Unity is married to maturity.

No church needs to remain in such a mess. There is a way out of this confusion and disarray. It starts by every person in the church speaking to every other person in the church. They are to speak the truth to each other. No doubt Paul has primarily the truth of the gospel in mind, but his words have a wider reference as well. Every word spoken is inspired by love; nobody is seeking his own interests, but the welfare of all.

Where nothing but truth is spoken and only love reigns, there spiritual growth takes place. Out of concern for others, each one passes on what he himself knows of God's Word and ways. In this way no area of spiritual life is left untouched. The process of conformity to Christ goes on apace, and his headship over the body becomes an experienced fact.

Yes, the local church is his body (4:16). In that body every organ has its own unique place while being at the same time co-ordinated with every other organ. All the organs have something particular to contribute to the welfare of the whole. Where each part does its bit, the whole body grows and is strengthened, and Christ's spirit of love pervades it all.

We should not be discouraged if we cannot master every single detail of Paul's picture. His overall message is crystal clear. A church is a body where each member lives for the well-being of the whole. Nobody thinks of himself but does what he can, however modest, to enrich the others. Love is the energy which activates every nerve.

Where this happens the body grows. It becomes more like its Head and operates in fuller submission to him. As it grows, so does its co-ordination. The organs work better and better together. Unity and maturity are vitally linked to each other and can never be separated.

Today, spiritual maturity is often presented as an individual affair. This is a grave misunderstanding. Physical organs do not mature in isolation from each other. The only maturing that ever takes place is in the context of a growing body. Where organs do not work for each other's good, growth is inevitably stunted. Where each one does its share the whole body grows, **'for the edifying of itself in love'** (4:16).

Nobody is serious about spiritual growth if he flits from church to church. The same is true of those who restrict themselves to those aspects of church life which appeal to them, or who are irregular in their attendance, passive rather than participating, poor in offering hospitality, limited in their friendships, content to leave the tasks to others, or who manifest their 'me first' attitude in other ways. The passage we have studied calls on such people to repent!

There is a final point we must make before leaving this section.

There is a lot of talk today about living the Christian life at home, or in the world. These subjects are vital and Paul's epistle to the Ephesians will cover them shortly. Why does Paul not tackle them straight away? It is because he knows we will never make much progress in those areas until we have first learned to live the Christian life *in the church.* Those who fail there fail everywhere. They also hold back the spiritual development of others.

'I, therefore, the prisoner of the Lord, beseech you to lead a life worthy of the calling with which you were called' (4:1).

10.
Christian living (1)

Please read Ephesians 4:17-32

We are in that part of his letter where Paul tells us that Christians live differently from other people. They behave in a certain way towards each other, and this we considered when we studied 4:1-16, which dealt with the unity of the church. In the passage before us, and also as far as 5:21, the apostle tells us how believers live in the world. He will cover such themes as their personal standards, their attitudes and their speech. We can put the whole of what he says under the general title of 'Christian living'.

Why this teaching is to be taken seriously

'**This I say, therefore, and testify in the Lord...**' (4:17) is how Paul introduces this subject. The word translated 'testify' can just as well be rendered 'insist'. 'I am speaking to you and insist in the name of the Lord that you pay attention to what I say,' says Paul.

It is the apostle to the Gentiles who is speaking. He did not give himself this office, but was appointed to it by none other than the Lord Jesus Christ. He has a right to give dogmatic teaching and to insist that we listen, for he speaks with the full authority of the Lord. As we have seen more than once, to listen to his teaching is to listen to Christ speaking; but to reject or ignore him is to do the same to the one who sent him.

Take this teaching seriously! Here is the will of the Lord Jesus Christ for your daily life! One of the sins of our day is that many people give more attention to what they see in visions than they do to the plain teaching given by Christ in his Word. But God's will is never now revealed in visions, however convincing they may be. If you want to know how to please Christ in this world, you must come to such passages as the one we have just opened.

Another reason for taking this teaching seriously is found in verse 30: **'And do not grieve the Holy Spirit of God, by whom you were sealed for the day of redemption.'** We learned about this sealing in chapter 1. We saw that a seal is a sign of ownership. Sealing is not something the Holy Spirit does. He is himself the seal. God has put his sign of ownership on all believers without exception by giving to them his Spirit.

If some believers had been sealed while others had not, this verse would be nonsense. We would have to assume that the only believers capable of grieving the Spirit were those who had experienced some superior blessing! As it is, all who are heading for the 'day of redemption' have been sealed. That day is the end of the world when believers will receive their resurrected bodies, be acquitted at the judgement and will enter into the full and unspoilt enjoyment of the heavenly blessings that Christ's redeeming blood has obtained for them. This will be the privilege of all those who carry God's mark of ownership. The seal guarantees that no child of God will be overlooked on that day. Every Christian will arrive safely in heaven!

Yes, each Christian is indwelt by the Holy Spirit. It follows that whenever he thinks, speaks or acts in an unholy way, he grieves that glorious person. What! Grieve the one who convinced us of our sin and misery, enlightened our minds to understand the gospel, brought us safely to the Saviour in repentance and faith, has kept us believing to this hour, inspires our hope of heaven and will give life to our dead bodies at the last day? Who would want to do such a thing?

Years ago, the streets of our large British cities were teeming with homeless children whose experience of life could be summed up in two words: grime and crime. Let's say you took one of these children into your family, surrounded him with love and godliness, educated him, and taught him to be clean, courteous and honest. How would you feel if he still sometimes found pleasure in grime and crime? And what if he went back to it altogether? Do we now understand why Paul's teaching must be taken seriously?

Why Christians cannot live as other people do (4:17-24)

In fact, Christians simply cannot live the same way as other people do. A Christian at school just cannot behave like his non-Christian friends. In the office or factory, in the home and neighbourhood, in public or in private, no believer is able to live in the same way as his unbelieving counterparts. It cannot be done.

Why is this? Paul's teaching can be summarized in a single sentence: You cannot be the same as other people because you are not the same as other people! It is as simple as that. The Bible does not say to us, 'Become something different!' Rather, it says, 'You *are* different. Be in practice what you are in fact.'

It is because unconverted people have a certain sort of mind that they live in the way they do. But we have had our minds changed. We are new people. It is clear, then, that we just have to live in a new way. Let us see how Paul brings all this out.

1. He looks at the unconverted (4:17-19)

v. 17: 'Don't walk like the other Gentiles. What are they like? Well, their chief characteristic is that they have futile minds. Their minds are set on things of no real value.'

It is true, isn't it? What unconverted people want more than anything is an untroubled life with an abundant supply of money and pleasurable experiences. But when we all come to stand before God's judgement seat, it will be seen that none of these things is of any real worth at all. So we, as believers, have a different scale of values. We simply cannot live like those whose values are worthless. This is the force of the apostle's argument.

v. 18: 'Their understanding is darkened by sin. They cannot see what is staring them in the face — for example, that creation declares the existence and power of the invisible God. Therefore they are far, far away from him, and deprived of spiritual blessings and privileges. This is because of the ignorance which is *in* them. It is not that they became benighted. They have been like this since birth. They are like this by nature. And they cannot change themselves, for they have hearts of stone.'

This is a very profound analysis of the unconverted heart. How is it that an unconverted scientist, examining this universe with all its intricacy and balance, can remain unmoved, while one who is a Christian falls before his Maker, admiring his wisdom, design and loveliness? How is it that unbelievers look at the cross, and walk away, while we gaze through our tears at what the Lord Jesus Christ did there? It is because of the petrification of their hearts — hearts which are incapable of beating in a spiritual world. Devoid of God in their understanding, unbelievers are devoid of him in their living. We are not like that, and we cannot live as they do.

v.19: 'What is inside shows itself outside. Having hearts of stone, they have no spiritual sensitivity. Nothing holds them back from doing whatever appeals to their physical appetites. They do whatever they want, even if it is unclean. They live to satisfy and to please themselves, however impure it may be. When they have had what they want, they then want more of it.'

If you doubt the truth of what Paul is saying, consider the television programmes which people watch in their own homes and family circle. Think of the language they tolerate and the immorality which is watched, supposedly for entertainment. This is what they feed their minds on, even if social pressures keep them from doing many of the things themselves. They even derive pleasure from witnessing gratuitous violence. The scale of values and code of behaviour to which they expose themselves is one which leaves God out completely. He is not there in their lives, even when they are being pleasant and neighbourly.

There is nothing in the Bible which suggests that a believer may not own a television. We must not let this area of Christian liberty lead us off the subject. Paul's point is that the unconverted leave God out of all they think and speak and do. We are not like that. So we cannot behave as they do.

2. He looks at Christians (4:20-24)

vv. 20-21: 'Being a Christian isn't just a matter of learning propositions but of learning *Christ,* the very embodiment of truth. If you have truly learned him, you will not have learned from him to live in the way we have been talking about.'

There is a world of difference between learning a lesson and learning a person. Christianity is more than grasping a set of truths which can be written on paper. It is all to do with knowing a person

— trusting, following and loving him. It is neither from our fallen nature nor from others that we learn how to behave. We learn it from him. And those who have not learnt it from him must doubt whether they belong to him at all.

v. 22: 'Well then, when you came to Christ, what did you learn? The first thing you learned was repentance. You learned to put off the old way of living. You ceased to be the person that you were. You can talk about your pre-conversion life as your "old self" or "old man". What a corrupt life that was, dominated as it was by strong and deceitful desires to which you constantly gave in!'

v. 23: 'Then you were made new inwardly. You were changed inside. The very spirit of your mind was transformed, making it impossible to be again what you once were.'

v. 24: 'At conversion you put off the old self and put on the new one. The "old man" has gone and the new one has come. Just as Adam was first made in the image of God, so you were remade in his image. The new "you" is one that longs for righteousness and holiness. Changed so wonderfully by God, you want to be like him.'

There are no imperatives in these verses. Paul gives no commands and makes no suggestions. Those who read the passage quickly, or who come to it with set ideas, often fail to realize this. The apostle is not telling us what *should* happen, but what *has* happened! Conversion is a moral transformation. The proof that you are converted is that your life has been changed. And it is precisely because it has changed that you can no longer live like those who remain unconverted.

The specific ways in which Christian behaviour is different
(4:25-32)

It is one thing to say that a Christian's life is changed; it is another to spell out precisely what this means in practice. This is what Paul does now. Every Christian is a new person. But not every Christian is living exactly as he should do. He needs to be told and reminded what he must finish with and what should be found in its place.

v. 25: 'Finish with lying. Put it away, in all its forms, for ever. Replace it with the truth. Every believer is to speak only truth to every person he meets...'

Lying is speaking untruthfully, with the intention of misleading or deceiving, and it has many forms. Any words which set out to convey a false impression are lies. This includes exaggeration, half-truths, and so-called 'white lies' — falsehoods uttered in the interest of tact or politeness. It also includes casuistry, that is, reasoning which is apparently correct, but actually false. Christians have been remade after the image of the God of truth. Their speech is to be taken up with what is true, genuine, actual and factual.

But when we paraphrased verse 25 a few moments ago, we did not finish it. It closes with a reason. We are not to lie, asserts Paul, **'for we are members of one another'**.

What does he mean? John Chrysostom, the golden-mouthed preacher of the fourth century, explained it like this: 'If the eye sees a serpent, does it deceive the foot? If the tongue tastes what is bitter, does it deceive the stomach?' When your eye sees a snake on the footpath it does not tell lies to the foot which is about to tread on it. It does not say that it is just a walking stick that someone has dropped. It tells the foot to turn round in a hurry and run the other way!

If the eye lied the body would die. If the tongue, tasting poison, told the stomach to expect a sweet delicacy, both tongue and stomach would perish. Every time we are untruthful, we destroy not only the person we are speaking to, but ourselves, too, 'for we are members of one another'.

vv. 26-27: 'Lying is not the only thing that is to be put away for ever. So is sinful anger. By all means be angry, but never in a sinful way, and never for long. Anger must certainly never be carried over from one day to the next. Don't ever play into the hands of the devil.'

Anger, in and of itself, is not wrong. Our Lord Jesus Christ was angry on a number of occasions during his public ministry. But we may only be angry at the things with which God is angry, and only ever for the same reason — that holiness has been outraged and God's universe spoiled even further.

Anger which is pure is a very rare thing. Even our holiest emotions and words are spoiled by sin. But even where anger *is* legitimate, it is not to last for long. We are not to go to bed and brood.

Righteous anger, like the manna from heaven, breeds worms if it is kept overnight. There are too many worms to count — bitterness, revenge, malice, spite, an unforgiving spirit, sharpness, grudges, hostility, irritability ... the list could go on and on. We are to wake each morning with no feelings of hurt *at all* carried over from the day before. If not, we shall be in a situation which the devil will definitely exploit. Unchristlikeness and unbrotherliness will take up residence in our hearts, and who knows where that will lead? No Christian is ever to let this happen, says the inspired apostle.

v. 28: 'And there is something else that you must finish with: stealing. Don't ever do it again! But it is not enough to stop something bad; you must start something good. Get to work, and meet your needs by honest toil. Stop looking for an easy life. And remember this: God expects you not only to meet your own needs, but also to use your earnings to help those in want.'

vv. 29-31: 'Not only actions must be put right, but words too. Get rid of the idea that your mouth exists for your benefit. No! It exists for the betterment and benefit of others. That is why God gave it and that is how it should be used. Nothing bad should ever come out of it. You should speak with your hearers in mind, and always and only with a view to doing them good and to advancing them spiritually. Bitterness, rage, annoyance, aggressiveness, defamation, malice — these things, in all their forms, are permanent outlaws to Christian speech.'

v. 32: 'Don't stop at getting just your words right. The Christian is to be distinguished by a whole new set of attitudes. Let every believer be friendly and affectionate to every other believer. Be warm and gentle with each other, not just outwardly but in your hearts. Others will certainly wrong you and I am not asking you to forget what they have done. Instead of forgetting, forgive. Behave towards them as if they had never done it, just as God in Christ also forgave you.'

Christian character is a very down-to-earth affair. The new man or woman whom God has made does not have a shining face and walk around with an ethereal goldfish bowl over his head. He does not send a tingle down the spine of those who meet him. He is not known for his sweet smile and marvellous charm. Integrity is his hallmark. In his life he is truthful, self-controlled, unselfish, honest, hard-working and wholesome. He enriches others wherever he goes. The attitudes which inspire him are markedly different to those he nursed in his unconverted days. This is because he has now been to the cross. God has forgiven him every sin that he ever committed against him — but, oh, at what cost! Forgiveness is his solely because of the shed blood of Christ.

The believer remembers how kind God has been to him, how very, very tender! His crimes are certainly written in the memory of the omniscient God. But this God treats him as if he had never sinned at all! He does not blame the Christian for anything! How then can this Christian continue to bear grudges against those who have wronged him? When he looks at the cross, he can only forgive them, just as he himself has been forgiven.

Christ has died, and the Christian's 'old self' died with him. Christ has risen, and with him the Christian rose to newness of life. Union with Christ is what makes a Christian a Christian. It is also what makes it impossible for him to live as he used to.

11.
Christian living (2)

Please read Ephesians 5:1-21

Christians, being new people, live differently from other people, not only when they are together (4:1-16) but also at all other times (4:17-32). This is the theme which is continued in the section we have now come to study.

To enter more easily into Paul's teaching here, there is an introductory point we need to grasp: the Christian life is a *walk*.

Having told his readers to follow God, Paul instructs them to **'walk in love'** (5:2), to **'walk as children of light'** (5:8) and to **'walk circumspectly'** (5:15). These three references to walking divide our passage quite naturally into three sections: the Ephesians must walk in love, in light and in wisdom.

The Christian life is a walk. To stress the need for self-discipline and perseverance, the apostle does sometimes describe the believer as an athlete (e.g. 1 Cor. 9:24; Gal. 2:2). But that is not his image here, because the purpose of this passage is different. We must not think of the Christian life as a run. Those who went to schools where cross-country runs were compulsory will remember what they were like! Sometimes you ran well, but at other times slowly. Sometimes you did not run at all, but sat down to rest. Sometimes you gave up completely. There was no telling what you would be like on any given day. God does not want us to live the Christian life like that. The wonderful thing about walking is that it is steady. There is a certain consistency about it. You keep up the same pace mile after mile. The picture, then, is well chosen. God wants us to be steady, consistent, always the same.

Walking is better than running. Those who run soon get tired. But the walker can keep going and keep going and keep going. His progress is a lot less dramatic, but at least it is certain. Which is better, a Christian life which is dramatic or one which is dependable? One which advances by fits and starts, or one of measurable, reliable progress?

Paul's use of the verb 'walk' makes it clear what God wants from us. 'Sameness' is a word which this modern age despises. It is, however, something which God values very highly. Whether we are on our own or with others, at peace or in pain, at work or at play, among Christians or pagans, it is God's will that we should always be the same, as far as our personal attitudes and behaviour are concerned.

How few can be depended upon to be like that! A spiritually advancing 'sameness' is a very rare sight indeed. But it will be less rare if we take to heart this passage. Here we may learn to walk well.

Walk in love (5:1-7)

To make his point, Paul uses a beautiful and simple illustration (5:1-2). Walking along a path are a group of children from the same family. They come to a point where they do not know which way to go. What are they to do? Which direction should they take? 'Follow Father,' says the apostle Paul. Those two words summarize the whole of verse 1.

Those words also summarize the core of our Lord's teaching in the Sermon on the Mount. Do you want to know how to treat people who are unkind to you? Follow your Father who is actively good to the just and unjust alike (Matt. 5:43-45). This principle is to guide our every action: 'You shall be perfect, just as your Father in heaven is perfect' (Matt. 5:48). Follow Father!

We are God's **'dear children'** (5:1). Unfortunately children, even when they are walking behind their parents, are prone to bicker and squabble. Those in God's family are never to be like that. They are to **'walk in love'** (5:2).

The word 'love' here is once more the Greek word *agapé*. It denotes love which spares no pains to promote the good and well-being of others. It is the self-giving love which Christ had for us and which took him to the cross. Calvary was horrific. But, more than the Old Testament offerings whose ascending smoke was sweet and pleasant to God, Christ's sacrifice on the cross was overwhelmingly pleasing to his Father. This sacrifice cannot ever be repeated. But Christ's love can be reflected in the way God's children treat each other. How much that would please the Father!

'But, Father,' says one of the children, 'look at those people over there. Look where they're walking! They are going down the path of sex before marriage and other sexual practices you forbid. It is the path of impurity and the desire for more...'

'Do not even *talk* of going that way,' comes the reply. 'Could people set apart to walk my path with me do such a thing, or even contemplate it? What could be more improper or unfitting?' (5:3).

'Father,' says another child, 'look where those people are walking now! They've taken the disgusting path of indecency, nonsensical and godless chatter, and dirty jokes...'

'My children, that will never be the right path for you. Those who are following a holy God cannot walk or speak in an unholy way. The way forward and upward for you is the giving of thanks. That is the right track' (5:4).

'Here is something you should know and never forget. The path of immorality and impurity certainly exists. So does the path of setting your heart on the possessions, property or experiences of others. This is idolatry, because it means giving these things the place in your life which rightly belongs to God alone. But no one who takes these paths will ever end up in the kingdom of Christ and God' (5:5).

'Those paths do not lead there, despite what people say. They will use all sorts of clever and persuasive words to get you to go along that road with them. They will tell you that no harm will come of it. Do not be taken in. The sins of which they speak so glowingly are precisely the sins which anger God and which he is certain to judge' (5:6).

If this is so, why do unconverted people do these things? It is because they are not following the Father. They are **'the sons of disobedience'** (5:6). How, then, can the Father's children behave as they do? The sins which the world puts at the top of its league are the very sins which cause people to be damned. Christians must have nothing to do with these things! (5:7).

In this first paragraph, then, the apostle has made it clear that there is a way for a believer to walk, and there is a way for him *not* to walk. He has also made it clear which is which.

Walk in light (5:8-14)

But it is not enough to walk in love for our Father and for each other. We must also **'walk as children of light'** (5:8).

Again and again our daily papers tell us of tragedies on mountains. Many of these take place because people walking in dangerous conditions are not always given sufficient training and a proper briefing. All experienced fell-walkers know what to do if they are still outside when night falls. They must stop. A path which appears safe in the dusk looks very different indeed the next morning! Broad daylight shows us what we could never see at night; some paths lead to certain ruin.

Why do unconverted people rush along the road to damnation? It is because they cannot see the danger. They do not see anything in its true light. They are in the dark — about God, about sin and its consequences, about our Lord Jesus Christ and about salvation. Not only are they in the dark, but they are actually *darkness* (5:8). They cannot see the right way to go and therefore fall to their destruction.

Paul reminds us that we were once like them (5:8). But this is no longer the case. Not only are we now 'children of light', but we are actually **'light in the Lord'**. How can we even consider walking along paths which the light reveals to be fatally dangerous? Believers simply cannot walk the same way as unconverted people. Those who are not the same cannot *be* the same.

The light of God's Spirit has shone in our lives, and the effect on us is as visible as fruit on a tree (5:9). Instead of the bad, we now love what is good. We steer clear of what is wrong, to do what is right. Falsehood we hate and we set our minds on what is true. We have been changed right round. We have been converted! All that interests us now is to please the Lord who has saved us (5:10). We want to follow Father, who is perfectly good and right and true. That is the path for us. The light we have received has convinced us of the idiocy of going any other way.

Yes, all other paths are fruitless (5:11). They come to nothing. They are valueless and we are to have nothing to do with them. Instead of going down such dark paths, we are to expose them. We are to show them up for what they are. This does not mean that believers are to spend their days constantly telling other people off. Nothing is more likely to put people's backs up and to give the impression that we consider ourselves better than others. How, then, are we to obey this command to **'have no fellowship with the unfruitful works of darkness, but rather expose them'**? (5:11).

Paul gives us the answer in verses 12 and 13. If we see someone going along a path which will kill him, there are a number of things we can do. The best is to shed light on the road that the person is taking, so he can see for himself where it will lead him. Words can do this, which is why the apostle himself is using them. But some sins are so shameful that we should never even mention them. How can we expose the most degrading paths of all?

No one ever got rid of darkness by talking all night. Only light dispels darkness. The rising sun drives the night away and reveals how dangerous certain 'safe' paths really are. This dark world is in need of light and only Christians are able to supply it. They do this when they live lives which are radically different from those around them. A life of wholesome holiness soon makes it clear what a dangerous and unhappy business sin is.

Some people have concluded from verses 12-13 that we should never speak against sin. This cannot be a correct understanding, because the apostle Paul is obviously speaking against sin himself. But he is not ranting. Loud tirades against evil never do any good. Often they prove to be nothing but loud words uttered by insincere people who, engrossed by the sins they are denouncing, end up doing the very things which they claim to detest. A life of light is what is required. Why curse the darkness when you can light a candle? The Scriptures are calling us here to live so differently from everyone else that it is soon clear to all that all paths are ruinous, except God's way. One holy life in a factory or office will do more to dispel its darkness than a million words from a person who is no different from the rest. Most powerful of all, of course, is a genuinely godly life backing up courageous and winsome words.

But what is verse 14 about? Having given this teaching, why does Paul then say, **'Therefore he says: "Awake, you who sleep, arise from the dead, and Christ will give you light"'**?

These verses are not found anywhere in the Old Testament, and yet the apostle is obviously assuming that his readers know them well. The most likely explanation is that he is quoting a well-known hymn of the early church, probably one which was sung regularly at baptisms. These are the words which the new Christians would have heard as they came up out of the water after their symbolic burial.

By quoting this hymn here, what Paul is saying is this: 'I am not telling you anything new. You are not hearing anything different from what was emphasized when you were immersed as a new believer. That act underlined that the Christian life is all about finishing with sin and walking in newness of life; it is about sin being dead and buried, and about living in the light. What you have known from the beginning, I am stressing once again.'

Walk in wisdom (5:15-21)

Believers are to walk in love and to walk in light. They are also to walk in wisdom. Verse 15 reads, **'See then that you walk circumspectly, not as fools but as wise.'**

A cat walking along a wall into which pieces of glass have been embedded is walking 'circumspectly'. He is watching where he is putting his feet! Christians are to be equally watchful. They are to tread carefully. They are not to rush foolishly ahead and live as they please, but to wisely consider every step.

This cannot be done without a proper attitude to time (5:16). Evil is all around us, and there is hardly anything that so effectively leads people to commit evil as idleness. The devil really does find work for idle hands to do. Unplanned time is something to be ashamed of. How many Christians come home from work or school and do not know what they are going to do that evening! They say, 'We shall see what happens.' This is pagan talk and should be denounced for what it is. Life is full of opportunities to do good, and we should make the most of those opportunities. Time is something to be 'redeemed'. It is highly valued and bought up. This can be done only by thinking ahead. We must decide what direction we are going to take and where we are going to put our feet. This is what walking 'circumspectly' means and in concrete terms. Unplanned time means certain sin.

'Don't, then, behave like those who don't know any better. Set yourselves to understanding what the Lord wants' (5:17). What is God's will for your life? Have you tried to find out? Have you found out? What commitments does the Lord want you to take on? What commitments does he want you to drop? Whom does he want you to write to? Whom does he want you to visit? What Christian work does he want you to get involved in? What special studies should you undertake? What hobbies are legitimate? What proportion of your time should you spend at home? What amount of time should you spend in extra hours at work? All these questions we should be able to answer, because we have thought them out and prayed them through. We should not be unwise, but should have an understanding of what the Lord wants from us.

This said, Paul moves on to speak out against a particular sin of his time, and ours. It is the sin of drunkenness. **'And do not be drunk with wine,'** he says, **'in which is dissipation'** (5:18). The Christian is always to be in charge of himself. He is never to lose control, because this in turn leads to unrestrained self-indulgence and immorality. If you take the reins off a wild horse, who knows where it may run?

It is certainly obvious to all that verse 18 must not be applied too narrowly. If it is wrong to be drunk with wine, it is equally wrong to be drunk with beer. Some people are 'drunk' with the disco beat which blows their minds, causing them to switch off and freak out. Others take drugs. Who can number the commodities and influences which bend the mind? But those who follow the Lord Jesus Christ are never to be numbered with those who no longer have full command of their faculties. We cannot walk that way, because that is the way this lost world walks.

Instead of all this, the believer is commanded to be **'filled with the Spirit'** (5:18). This expression is used in a number of different ways in the New Testament, and taking the time to look at them is a most rewarding study. Here in Ephesians 6:18 it is a plural command, so it applies to every Christian. It is not an optional extra, but an obligation. It is also a passive command, so it speaks of letting something happen to us. And it is a present command. This means, in Greek, that it is something which is to happen to us all the time. In modern English we would translate Paul's instruction like this: 'All of you, go on letting yourselves be filled with the Spirit.'

Paul's use of the Greek language in verses 19-21 reveals that four things happen to those who are filled with the Spirit.

1. They *speak to one another*. They enjoy fellowship with each other in an atmosphere of praise. The Spirit does not divide them, but brings them ever closer together (5:19).

2.They *sing and make melody in their hearts* to the Lord. They have great thoughts about the God of Scripture and their hearts go out to him in joyful worship (5:19).

3. They *give thanks* always for all things to God the Father, in the name of the Lord Jesus Christ. They do not moan about anything that comes into their lives. They see that their Father has sent it and they thank him for it all. In their approach to him, they rely entirely on the mediation of their Saviour 5:20).

4. They *submit to one another* out of reverence for God. Each one considers the others to be better than he is. No one believes he is the greatest. All are concerned to treat fellow-believers in a way which would please God (5:21).

The passage we are studying has told us a great deal about how to live the Christian life. We can now summarize it in a sentence: **'Be filled with the Spirit!'** But how do we get filled?

Verse 18 makes everything clear. How does a person get drunk with wine? He drinks and drinks and drinks again, until what he has drunk takes control. The same principle applies in the spiritual realm. We must drink spiritual things until we are under the Spirit's influence. It is the Lord Jesus Christ who gives us the Spirit, and this is what he said in John 7:37-39: '"If anyone thirsts, let him come to me and drink. He who believes in me, as the Scripture has said, out of his heart will flow rivers of living water." But this he spoke concerning the Spirit, whom those believing in him would receive; for the Holy Spirit was not yet given, because Jesus was not yet glorified.'

Being constantly filled with the Spirit is a matter of constantly drinking. We are to go to Christ and to drink of him. We do this in prayer, listening to biblical preaching, studying God's Word for ourselves, engaging in Christian fellowship, meeting around the Lord's Table, and in every form of spiritual and devotional exercise. As the Spirit does his work through these means, we become more spiritual people, with the four results that we have just considered.

In this wicked world is there anything more striking and pleasant than seeing people walking day after day with God? By taking to heart what we have just studied, that walk may be ours.

12.
Christian living in the home

Please read Ephesians 5:22 - 6:9

The apostle Paul has made it clear that Christians live differently from other people. When they are together, their behaviour contrasts sharply with the social behaviour of the unconverted (4:1-16). When they are surrounded by the men and women of the world in daily life, their conduct remains distinct (4:17 - 5:21). Paul is now going to tell us that they also live in a radically different way at home (5:22 - 6:9).

It is fairly easy to live the Christian life at church. It is much more difficult to do so in the world. But the hardest place of all to live as a Christian is at home. This is why the apostle comes to this subject last of all.

Paul's treatment of this subject is fairly lengthy, and it might surprise you to discover that this commentary will devote only one chapter to it. But we have already spoken about missing the wood for the trees. If we get engrossed in details, we shall perhaps not grasp the full force of what the apostle is saying. To avoid this danger, we are going to extract from his teaching its four most important points. With these bold lines engraved in our minds, we shall clearly see what are the greatest principles of God's Word relating to Christian living in the home.

The Christian life has to be lived at home

For many years I lived in a house, but when I married, that house became a home! What makes a house into a home? A wife. This was a fact of which Paul was only too well aware, although he himself was not married. This explains why he begins his teaching on this subject by talking to wives (5:22-24,33). It is as if Paul was saying, 'If your home is going to be the sort of home that God wants to see, you are going to have to be the sort of *wife* that God wants to see!'

Now, for a wife to be a wife, what must there be? A husband. There cannot be wives unless there are husbands. They are addressed next (5:25-33). The apostle has more to say to them than he does to wives. In fact he has more to say to them than to any other group at home, for reasons which will become clear later. It is as if he was saying to them: 'If your home is going to be the sort of home that God wants to see, you are going to have to be the sort of *husband* that God wants to see.'

In most cases, though not all, it is not too long before a husband and wife find their home graced with children. These are the people to whom the apostle speaks next (6:1-3). We should note that when his letter was read to the church, Paul took it for granted that the children of the church would be present to hear him. They were not absent when the sermon was given. Paul's message to them was this: 'For the home to be all that God wants it to be, boys and girls must be the sort of *children* that God wants to see.'

Of course, it is the arrival of children that makes a married couple into parents. Husband and wife are now also 'Mum and Dad'. The word 'parents' is used in 6:1, but the apostle does not speak to them as such. His remarks about parenting are addressed only to the father of each family (6:4). Why is this? Why doesn't he speak to the mothers as well?

It is because Christ is the head of the man, who, in turn, is the head of his wife and home (see 1 Cor. 11:3). In God's plan, authority in the home is vested in the man, the husband, the father. It is he who, at the final judgement, will be held accountable for the quality and integrity of family life. This does not mean that mothers have no authority over their children. They have a claim to their children's obedience, as 6:1 makes plain. But their authority is delegated to them by their husbands, rather than something they have in their own right. It is not, then, an authority they can exercise when their husbands are at home. In God's institution of family life, it is fathers who are held finally responsible for the upbringing of their children.

Wives, husbands, children, parents — there is no one else to consider in a modern family. How different this is from the situation which prevailed when Paul wrote! In most cases there were other people living at home as well. These were the *slaves,* whom Paul speaks to in 6:5-8. Tens of thousands of the early believers were slaves, and from their number came some of the finest Christian leaders and preachers of the first century. It was essential that these believing slaves should also know how to live at home, where they spent almost all their time and did most of their work. For a home to be all that God wanted it to be, Christian slaves had to be a certain sort of slave.

The presence of slaves meant that very many Christian men wore more than two hats. Not only were they husbands and fathers; they were also *masters.* Paul addresses these men in 6:9. Without being sidetracked, it is important for us to realize that a man could still be a master, although he was a Christian. The Bible strongly condemns man-stealing, but it does not condemn slavery as such. In certain closely defined circumstances, one human being may own another. The Old Testament, in particular, makes this abundantly clear. Such slavery had almost nothing in common with the disgusting slave trade which blots European history, nor with the slavery still found in many pagan cultures today. Christian masters were to be careful not to be the same as other masters. Unless they were a certain sort of master, their home life could never be what God wanted it to be.

The Christian life has to be lived at home. This is the theme of the whole passage we are studying. Paul is not dealing with any other subject. We must not, then, take what he says to slaves and masters and apply it to modern employees and employers. The apostle is not discussing industry, but the home. The master - slave relationship of 2,000 years ago has very little in common with the organization of our work-places today. It is illegitimate to take verses completely out of their context and to apply them to situations which they were never intended to address.

Paul is talking about our homes. Why does he spend so much time on this subject? It is because it can be said of too many professing Christians: 'He is a saint abroad but a devil at home.' When they are with believers, such people are very plausible. Even at work, and in the world at large, they stand against wrong and appear to be true Christians. But what are they like at home? There they relax, with their defences down. As they put on their slippers they take off their mask. Their life at home is a disgrace. It is very different to the way they live outside. So much of it is unchristian.

The apostle sets his face against such inconsistency. Home is where we are known the best, misunderstood the most and are constantly open to scrutiny and criticism. But it is supremely here that the Christian life has to be lived, because it is here that the gospel is put to its severest test. If the gospel is unable to transform people at home, we must conclude that it is unable to transform people at all. Ungodly behaviour here shames the gospel. 'He whose light shines furthest, shines brightest nearest home.'

Not everyone at home has the same rôle

In our passage Paul addresses each person in the home separately, with no overlap. The only exception is at the end of verse 33. Apart from that, what he says to wives, husbands, fathers, slaves and masters is quite distinct. All these people live under the same roof. But the apostle gives them very different instructions.

Now, undoubtedly, wives enjoy certain privileges which are theirs, and theirs alone. The same could be said for each of the groups mentioned. But that is not Paul's theme here. He is not talking about privileges, but responsibilities. Each person in the family must clearly understand what are his or her responsibilities and duties, before he or she ever enquires about any privileges which might be his.

This fact tells us a great deal about Christian family life as God intends it to be. The home is not to be a place where any member asks, 'What can I get out of family life?' Not at all. The questions which each member is to ask and answer are rather: 'What is expected of me at home? What is expected of *me?*' The difference between these questions is the whole difference between the way a Christian and a non-Christian lives at home. Believers are new people. They therefore live in a new way. Like the Lord Jesus Christ whom they follow, they understand that their calling is not to take, but to give. This they must do, whatever it costs them personally.

But we must underline that the question to be answered is: 'What is expected of *me?*' What is expected of a wife is not what is expected of a husband. The same is true of children and fathers, and slaves and masters. There are distinct, separate and plainly defined rôles for each person in the household. They live together, but each one has his or her own set of duties.

The way for a Christian home to operate is not for me to ask what God expects of him, or of her, or of them, but to be clear what he expects of *me*. Homes are ruined when everybody criticizes everybody else's performance. The way forward is for each person to weigh up before God what are his or her own responsibilities, and to take them seriously. Homes are changed for ever when each person asks the others to help him do what God expects of him personally.

No one can exaggerate the importance of this approach. For example, when we consider more closely what God expects of wives, husbands reading this book will be tempted to ask how their wives are shaping up. Wives, on the other hand, will be tempted to close their hearts to what God's Word is saying, and to take comfort from the fact that their husbands will soon be having their turn! Such is the perversity of the human heart that we are always more interested in the performance of others than in our own. Family breakdown has already started when we criticize others for their failures, and stop examining ourselves in the light of God's Word, asking, 'What is expected of me?'

The rôle of each person is clearly defined

There can be no confusion about what is expected of each member of the family. God has made it so clear. To each person he has given just one main idea to remember.

The keyword for wives is **'submit'**. This is taught in 5:22-24,33. But what does that mean? It means that the wife puts herself entirely at the disposal of her husband. This is not something forced upon her. It is something which she does voluntarily out of respect for Christ. Everything that she is and has is for her husband. This includes, of course, her judgement, her intuition, her intellect, her gifts, her everything. She says to him, in effect: 'Here I am, here is what I am, here is what I have — and it is all for you.' In God's pattern for the family, this is the rôle of the wife. It is not so much to obey, as some wedding services have it, but to 'submit' to her husband (5:22), to be subject to him in everything (5:24) and to respect him (5:33).

The wife's rôle being to submit, we would expect husbands to be called to 'rule'. But they are not. Their rôle is not authoritarian. Their keyword tells them to **'love'**, as we see in verses 25-33.

The Greek language has many words for love. One of them refers simply to lust, and that is certainly not a word which Paul uses in this paragraph. Another carries the idea of warm, faithful friendship. Paul does not use that either, because it is not strong enough to convey accurately what a man's relationship to his wife should be. Once more, the apostle chooses the word *'agapé'*. This is the word which describes Christ's love for his people. It is love which operates through self-sacrifice. It is a giving love which seeks the welfare of the other, whatever the pain, whatever the cost and however great the difficulty. Where God's distinctives for family living are observed, the wife puts herself completely at the disposal of a man who wants nothing but her good, and who is making every sacrifice necessary to obtain it. Could such a couple be anything but wonderfully happy?

The keyword for children is **'obey'** (6:1). They must do what their parents tell them. And they must do it for no other reason than that their parents tell them to do it. Parents do not give themselves authority. Their right and duty to command their children is God-given. Any resistance to such authority is therefore rebellion against God himself. No doubt, as children grow towards maturity, their obedience also matures. In the life of a toddler, the 'honour' mentioned in verse 2 expresses itself in unquestioning obedience. When the child has become an adult, this 'honour' remains intact, but expresses itself quite differently, such as in the care and consideration which is to be given to elderly parents. Whatever their age and experience, children are to look up to their parents. Anything which causes them to do otherwise is a departure from God's law.

But what keyword shall we give to fathers, seeing that there is no clear word to fix on in 6:4? Paul insists that there is something which fathers are never to do: they are never to exasperate their children. Sometimes the discipline of a home brings a child to the point where he thinks he can do nothing right. Everything he does is wrong. The child cries out with a frustration which makes him angry with his parents and resentful of his upbringing. This is never to happen in a Christian home. Christian fathers are never to push their children to this point. Instead, they are to **'bring them up in the training and admonition of the Lord'** (6:4). A Christlike spirit is to reign in the family. Everything which is done at home, and all that is said there, is to gently and powerfully attract boys and girls to Christ. Even strong action and stern words are to work in this direction. The whole atmosphere of the home is to be conducive to spirituality. The father's rôle with respect to his children is to be an encourager. Now we have found his keyword. He is to *'encourage'*.

But what about the slaves? Verses 6:5-8 are easily summarized. What is required of them is consistent, good-natured obedience to their masters. That is the key concept. Christ is their true Master, and they are to behave towards their earthly masters as they would behave towards him! Such an instruction is simply expressed by the apostle. Obedience to it by countless believing slaves revolutionized the structure of Roman society, and paved the way for its eventual abolition of slavery.

And what does Paul say to slave-masters? (5:9). He reminds them that they are over others; this is what makes them masters. But they are also under somebody. They have their own Master. If they remember this, it will have a transforming effect on their lives. For example, they will give up threatening their slaves, because this does not please the Master to whom they themselves will one day give account. Their status in society does not entitle them to preferential treatment in Christ's court. The keyword for masters is thus *'answerability'*, because just as their slaves are answerable to them, so they are answerable to their Master in heaven.

Each member of the household, then, has his or her own keyword or concept. Let us now try to imagine a family where each member lives by what he or she has been told. The wife lives for her husband. The husband leads the home, and lives for his wife. The children are obedient. The father is a constant encourager, and even his anger is used to point the family to Christ. The slaves serve their master just as they would serve their Saviour and, in his treatment of the slaves, the master never does anything of which his Master would disapprove. Oh, this home is such a pleasant place to be in! What harmony! In this family there is a touch of heaven on earth.

How sadly different is the family where what we have studied is unknown or ignored! The wife puts herself first. The husband gives no spiritual lead, does not actively seek his wife's good and makes no sacrifices for her. The children pay no attention to what anyone says to them. The father vents his anger on anyone and anything which inconveniences him. The servants are disrespectful and dishonest. The master is self-important and shouts out constant threats. It only takes each person to forget his or her distinctive rôle for family life to become hellish.

Important reasons are attached to these instructions

No home is happy where God's directives for family living are put aside. This, in itself, is reason enough to take Paul's instructions seriously. Under divine inspiration he has given us a certain formula for happy family life. But it is not to this point that he appeals as he addresses each group of people. The reasons for his teaching are built on a much firmer foundation than that.

Why are wives to submit to their husbands, as to the Lord? (5:22). It is because this is in line with God's blueprint for the family. There is a pattern of headship written into God's universe, and this is to be reflected in the way family life operates. Not only so, but the way a husband and wife behave towards each other is to be a visual parable reflecting the relationship which exists between Christ and his church (5:23-24). The Bridegroom is the Head of his bride, whom he has saved, and she is to be submissive to him. The reasons why wives must submit to their husbands are thus substantial, spiritual and convincing.

Why must husbands love their wives? (5:25). To answer this, we must be aware of a spiritual reality (5:26-33). Christ sacrificed himself for his church. He gave himself for it, that it might be set apart for God. Each Christian testifies to having been thus cleansed and set apart when he is baptized, and the cleansing and sanctifying process is continued as Christ's Word does his work in him. One day the Saviour will take his bride to his home and she will be altogether glorious. There will be nothing to spoil her. She will be perfectly holy. He will do this because he is not something separated from her, but united to her. She is his body. This is why he looks after her in the loving and caring way that he does.

Men who are members of Christ's church are to proclaim this truth in the way that they behave towards their wives (5:26-33). The husband is the head of his wife and he is to be characterized by sacrificial love. He is to care for his wife's spiritual progress and total welfare. He is to remember that in marriage two have become one. He cannot behave towards his wife as if she were something separate from himself. Husband and wife are mysteriously united.

Her welfare and his cannot be distinguished. In living for her, he does not deprive himself of anything. Rather, he enriches himself. The whole relationship is to be a vibrant and obvious portrayal of the union of the Lord Jesus Christ and his people. These are the reasons which should persuade Christian husbands, of all people, to live by God's Word at home.

Why are children to obey their parents? (6:1). There is such a thing as absolute right and wrong. How do we know which is which? This is decided by God's character, reflected in his law. When we are talking about obedience to parents, we can say that 'this is right' (6:1). In addition, God blesses obedience (6:2-3). The command to honour father and mother is the first of the Ten Commandments to have a promise attached to it. Children do not lose out by obeying their parents, despite what they themselves might sometimes think. Modern peer pressure, and most television programmes, have got it wrong. Boys and girls should close their ears to these other voices and listen to God. Obedient children enjoy his smile and not his frown. They live! This experience is not something they have to wait for. They enjoy it here and now, on the earth. Where children are in any way responsible for their own weak and unhappy characters, they will always be found to be disobedient children. They have not learned to do anything on the sole ground that it is right. Tender human plants which grow on the soil of rebellion against God-given authority are inevitably poisoned.

Why are fathers to be encouragers? (6:4). Paul gives no clear-cut reasons here, but in the parallel passage in Colossians 3:21 he says, 'Fathers, do not provoke your children, lest they become discouraged.' God has constituted our world in such a way that parents are the greatest single influence on the life of their children. They can make them or break them. They can shape characters or ruin them. Teachers, neighbours, friends, brothers and sisters certainly play a significant part in forming the child's developing personality. But their power is nothing compared with that of parents. What a high calling is theirs! And in a biblically organized home, where the man is head under Christ, the influence of the father is supreme. Seeing that his input is most likely to be the factor which will decide what direction his child's character will take, let him take his awesome responsibility seriously!

Why are slaves to give their masters constant, good-natured obedience? (6: 5-8). Why are masters constantly to call to mind their own answerability? (6:9). It is because they now live in the real world. The present master-slave relationship is only temporary. Nobody is anybody's slave for ever. Masters will not always have people under them. But all believers are slaves of Christ, and he is the Master of all, be they enslaved or free at this moment. Slaves must certainly do the will of their earthly masters, but in such a way that they are in fact doing the will of their eternal Master, before whom they shall certainly appear. Masters may indeed instruct and rule their slaves, but can never be a law unto themselves. The master-slave relationship which exists on earth reflects a heavenly reality which must not be forgotten. The whole of our life and service is under constant scrutiny by the Lord himself. He will shortly and certainly call us all to account.

In his world, God has set up three institutions — the family, the state and the church. Of these three, the family was set up first, and the other two were initially contained within it. The family is thus very precious to God. He desires that its glory should be seen in the lives and experience of the people he has redeemed. This is why Christ's apostle speaks so fully about family life here.

If Christians live badly at home, they discredit the gospel in the worst manner possible. God intended that the home should be the first place where godliness should be seen, not the last. The sort of Christians we are at home is the sort of Christians we are really.

We close this chapter by stressing what we said at its beginning. It is not easy to live the Christian life at home. It is the hardest place of all. Our guard is down and we cannot escape from the searching gaze of those who know us through and through. Home is where others see us as we are. It is here that we speak so many unwise words and think so many uncharitable thoughts. It is here that our selfishness is most visible. It is the place where the devil attacks us most and is the scene of our worst failures. A few hours at home are enough to convince us all that we still have a very great deal of spiritual progress to make. But how can we learn to live honourably for Christ in an area where all have done so badly?

It is no mistake that the apostle goes straight from the theme of Christian living in the home to that of our spiritual welfare.

13.
Finally...

Please read Ephesians 6:10-24

We now come to the last paragraph of Paul's great letter, which begins with the word, **'Finally...'**

The letter's first three chapters have told us of the marvellous blessings we have in Christ. We are no longer what we used to be. We are radically different. And we are infinitely rich. The next three chapters have made one overall point: *being* different, we should *live* differently. We have been taught how to do this in the church, in the world and at home.

But such Christian living is not easy. In fact, it is a real battle. Paul would not have anyone believe otherwise. So it is that he closes his letter with his well-known teaching on the Christian's armour. As he dictated this paragraph, under house arrest at Rome, the apostle probably had a Roman soldier in the same room. He may even have been chained to him. The first person to hear the epistle to the Ephesians, other than Paul's secretary, was this living visual aid! What did he think as Paul described each piece of his armour and showed what was its spiritual equivalent? Did he also notice that Paul's style as he signed off his letter was rather like that of a general briefing his troops before battle?

I am very well aware of how great preachers of the past have tackled Paul's teaching on the Christian armour. Dr Martyn Lloyd-Jones preached for months on these verses and we are privileged to be able to read his rich teaching in his multi-volume exposition of Ephesians. The thoughts of the great Puritan William Gurnall are encapsulated in his immense book *The Christian in complete armour,* and all who take the time and effort to read this magnificent classic will be rewarded a hundred times over. Yet it remains sadly true that many people who have read these wonderful books have missed the real point of what Paul is saying here. They have never got hold of his main message.

This slim volume will never rival the great books we have just mentioned, though it might prepare someone to get into them. All we are going to do here is to consider the main thrust of Paul's closing words. We will summarize it under four headings.

We are soldiers ar war!

When I was in my teens, and still at school, I was a very keen army cadet. Each Thursday evening I would clean and press every part of my uniform, and on Friday I would go proudly through the streets of Chester to the parade. I looked like a soldier, was conversant with military procedures and discipline, could operate the latest weapons and signalling devices, and occasionally had to put myself out. But my military life was never dangerous and never lasted more than a few hours at a time. During most of the week I had no contact with the army at all.

How different is the life of a soldier at war! He is under arms both day and night. His every waking thought is concerned with the conflict in which he is engaged. There may be an encounter with the enemy at any moment. All his work is directly connected with the war effort. His eating, sleeping and relaxing serve only one purpose — to strengthen him for warfare. There is no time when he ceases to be a soldier and there is no limit to what he may be required to do. His life is one of sacrifice, difficulty, danger, pain, tears, frustration and, perhaps, death.

This is the picture which Paul uses to speak of the Christian life! Being a Christian is not a hobby. It is not something in which we can get involved for only part of the week. It demands all that we are, all of the time. It is our life. We are soldiers at war. Everything is difficult and dangerous. It is a battle. All that we do is worth it, as we have so constantly seen in Paul's letter. But this does not lessen the reality of the war.

Look at the language the apostle uses. It is all so military. He calls us to **'be strong'** (6:10). He tells us that we need divine strength for the conflict (6:10). We have something to **'stand against'** (6:11), and to **'wrestle against'** (6:12). Flaming arrows are being shot at us (6:16), but we are to stand our ground (6:13-14), to take up our swords (6:17) and go to war!

It is time to stop misleading people when we present the gospel to them. The blessings of the Christian life are indescribable. Chapters 1-3 have made that more than clear. But every day and hour bring us new hardships and difficulties. This is a fact of which we are only too well aware. It is dishonest to hide it from those who are not yet believers. Our Lord Jesus Christ spoke openly of the cost of discipleship to those who were thinking of following him. So must we.

Our warfare is spiritual

What is the main aim of war, of any war? It is to hold your ground and to capture that of your enemy by defeating him. War is both defensive and offensive. We, as Christian believers, have ground to hold, both in the realms of what we believe and how we behave.

Who can count the enemies plotting against us in the area of belief? Roman Catholicism has so captured the media that the average person is coming to believe that it represents authentic Christianity. Liberalism has successfully invaded the major denominations so that the Bible is no longer submitted to as the inerrant Word of God, and man is the centre of all things. Ecumenism proclaims that doctrine is not as important as was once thought, and that churches should play down their differences so as to present a united front to an unbelieving world. The charismatic movement devalues the Bible by saying that God speaks outside it. Neo-evangelicalism believes that it is possible to hold on to the true gospel without insisting on truths which embarrass modern people, such as the six-day creation, or the conscious everlasting punishment of the unconverted.

The list is endless. Cults which deny the eternal deity of Christ knock on our doors or stop us in the street. Whole nations are still enslaved by false religions. The West abandons its Christian heritage a little more each day, opening its doors ever wider to atheism, nihilism, materialism and the theory of evolution — God is an influence, man is an accident produced by time plus chance, life has no meaning, so set your heart on living as comfortably as possible.

These are just some of the views which are taking over people's minds. Modern thinking is increasingly hostile to the gospel. It is in this context that we have to hold our ground, and win people from these false views by defeating them.

Not only so, but we must also hold our ground in the realm of behaviour. What God's Word defines as sexual sin is now regarded as normal conduct. Human life is no longer sacred — society approves of the killing of unborn boys and girls, refuses to condemn the 'merciful' killing of its chronically ill and elderly citizens, and does not think that deliberate murder is horrific enough for the murderer to be deprived of his own life. Hard work is for fools. To have strongly held principles is to be a fanatic. And the culture which has surrounded so much pop music has persuaded two generations that almost any behaviour is legitimate, as long as it leaves you feeling 'great'. All this, and much more, is an assault upon what God has revealed about how we are to live. Everything we believe in this area is under threat. How can we hold our ground? And is advance still possible?

Yet the ideas and practices we have mentioned are not our real enemies. **'We do not wrestle against flesh and blood,'** insists Paul (6:12). We are not at war with Roman Catholics, liberals, Jehovah's Witnesses or evolutionary scientists. We do not fight adulterers, gays, pop stars or the managers of abortion clinics. We are not in conflict with any man or woman. So who, then, are our enemies? We are **'against principalities, against powers, against the rulers of the darkness of this age, against spiritual hosts of wickedness in the heavenly places'** (6:12).

Why do people believe ideas which are not true? Why do they persist in behaving in a way which God condemns? It is because their minds are controlled by other personalities.

Who, precisely, are these personalities? The Epistle to the Ephesians has already spoken of the existence of the devil (2:2, 4:27). He is a personal, invisible and powerful spirit who controls the minds of the unconverted (2:2). He does this by means of his countless agents mentioned in verse 12. They, like him, are evil spirits. They are organized into various ranks, some of the names of which are given here. The devil himself is over them all. The darkness of this age is to be attributed to these awful beings. The invisible dimension is infested with them.

Why do so many scientists teach evolution as a fact, when it is only a theory? How can anyone be callous enough to extinguish human life in the womb? What leads people to suppress their innate knowledge of God and to declare themselves atheists? From where do men and women get the idea that there is no absolute right and wrong, when their conscience tells them otherwise? The gospel is true and can be known to be true — so what leads people to ignore, reject or oppose it?

There is only one answer to these questions, and to all questions like them. Men and women have been blinded. Their thought processes and powers of reason have been perverted by evil powers. Our real quarrel is not with our fellow human beings, but with the satanic spirits who have degraded and enslaved them. Diabolical personalities control their minds.

Battle is joined, and that battle is for the mind. Will God liberate it, or will it remain in enemy hands? We are to gain ground from the devil without giving in to him ourselves. He will do all he can to make us stand down on our beliefs and standards, while we will do all we can to bring people out of error and oppression into the glorious liberty of the gospel. The battle is on. It rages every day, every hour and everywhere. We are always in the thick of it. Everything we have, and are, and do, is to be part of the war effort. It is to occupy our thoughts, direct our energies, and be the consuming passion of our lives. We are soldiers at war, and our warfare is spiritual.

There is no need for us to be conquered

God himself has provided us with a complete protection, so that nothing the devil throws at us might bring us down. All we have to do is to put this armour on (6:11,13).

We do not need to fear the enemy. There is nothing about modern beliefs and behaviour which should cause us to turn tail and run. Far from it! We are, rather, to square up to the adversary, to get our courage from God, to join battle, and to trust that God's almighty power will cause us to prevail (6:10). We must have a mind to fight. If we do not, not even the complete armour which God has supplied will do us any good. But if we face the troops ranged against us, with every piece of armour in place, the devil will get nowhere with us (6:13).

There were five pieces of armour that no Roman soldier ever dared to neglect. If he did, he knew that he was virtually certain to die in battle. Paul now mentions these five pieces of protection in the order that a Roman soldier would have put them on (6:14-17).

The first thing a soldier donned was his protective apron, or *girdle* (6:14). It was like a thick leather belt from which hung down a number of thongs, often with metal plates attached to them. This girdle protected the lower part of the soldier's body while at the same time giving him freedom of movement. It was particularly effective against horizontal swipes of the sword.

In the same way the Christian believer is to bind himself round with **'truth'** (6:14). It is the first thing he must be sure of before he goes to battle. What is in mind here is the objective truth of the Bible. God has revealed to us all that we need to know of him, and what duty he requires of us. This revelation has been written down and constitutes the Holy Scriptures. God's Word is truth (John 17:17). We are to know and believe all that God has said. Who can enjoy protection from error, and who can advance against it, without being protected by truth?

Once his girdle was secure, the Roman soldier fitted on his *breastplate* (6:14). This was a very tough leather smock which covered his chest, and sometimes his back as well. As often as not, the front part was reinforced with metal. If the breastplate was not securely fastened, the soldier knew that he was unlikely to survive even the briefest encounter with the enemy.

The Christian's breastplate is **'righteousness'** (6:14). In the New Testament this word has two meanings. It is possible that the apostle Paul has both of them in mind here. It can refer to right living. To know that something is right, and not to do it, is to leave a gaping hole in your armour. The Christian is to be sure to 'put on' righteousness (6:14). How else will he be able to stand true in a world where there is so much ungodly behaviour?

But there is more to it than that. 'Righteousness' also refers to the perfect life of Christ which is put on the account of every believer. The devil is always telling us that we are 'no good'. We know he is right and we fall into discouragement. The fight goes out of us. What are we to do? We are to remember that our acceptance with God does not depend upon how well we are doing in our Christian lives. It is in no way linked to our performance. We are welcomed by the Father because our sins were all punished when Christ died for us, and his righteousness imputed to us makes us glorious in his sight. When we 'put on' such a way of thinking, all the devil's attempts to discourage us come to nothing.

After his girdle and breastplate, the Roman soldier puts on his *footwear* (6:15). In most climates he wore hobnailed sandals, attached to his feet and ankles by intertwining strips of leather. The secure fastening and the nails combined to give him the firm footing which is so essential in combat. A man fighting for his life does not want to slip and slide!

We, too, must have a firm footing if we are going to fight well in our spiritual warfare. We find it in 'the prepared foundation of the gospel of peace', as we can translate the end of verse 15. We need to reflect on the fact that we are at peace with God. We should treasure it up in our minds. We believe God's truth, we are righteous in Christ, and so we are at peace with God! There is nothing between me and him. All obstacles to my enjoying him have been removed. He was angry with me, but that anger has now been turned away, having been carried by the Lord Jesus Christ. Peace prevails. Nothing can destroy it. No, there is nothing in the whole creation which is able to separate me from the love of God which is in Christ Jesus our Lord (Rom. 8:39). However fierce the conflict, the person who stands on the peace which the gospel brings will never be moved. He is more than prepared for battle.

What came after the girdle, breastplate and sandals? It was the *shield* (6:16). Different regiments of the Roman army used different sorts of shields, but Paul has in mind the design which was used by the majority. From the front it appeared rectangular, but it was curved in such a way that it also protected a good deal of the soldier's sides. About four feet high, and thirty inches across, it completely obscured a crouching man from view. Often the enemy would shoot arrows whose bitumen-covered shafts were a mass of flame. Soldiers who hid behind their shields had little to fear from these burning missiles, which burned out fairly quickly. Groups of soldiers could put their shields together in such a way that they carried a protective roof which resembled a giant tortoise. Whatever the enemy fired at them had no effect. It came to nothing. The 'tortoise' was even able to go right up to the walls of enemy cities without much fear of harm. Such was the value of the Roman shield and the skill of those who bore them.

Faith is the Christian's shield. The devil can do nothing against it. His worst attacks are frustrated. Faith offers complete protection and makes advance possible. Where there is faith, there is nothing to fear. And what is faith? It is believing what God has said, for no other reason than that he has said it. It is taking God at his word. It is accepting his teaching, obeying his commands, heeding his threats and laying hold of his promises. Where there is faith, defeat is unknown. The soldier who has it is never floored by anything. Faith is invincible.

Last of all, the soldier put on his *helmet*. In the same way, the Christian believer is to **'take the helmet of salvation'** (6:17). But what does this mean? Isn't the Christian already saved?

To answer this, we need only to remember that God's Word uses the word 'salvation' in three ways. It is used of what God has done for us in the past, where it refers particularly to Christ's saving work on the cross and our experience of it. It also refers to what God is doing for us now: he is treating us as his children and is changing us in heart and behaviour by his Holy Spirit. But the word 'salvation' is also used of what God is certainly going to do for us in the future. Raised from the dead, acquitted at the final judgement, we shall spend eternity in the new heavens and earth. There, in perfect holiness and happiness, we shall fully enjoy God for ever. This is what the apostle is talking about here. The helmet is to do with the head, and he is telling us to keep the coming salvation in mind. We shall not be on the battlefield for ever. The conflict will soon be over. Before long, we shall be in heaven. It is not hard to fight well if you keep thinking about that.

What, then, is the complete armour which God gives to the Christian? How shall we sum it all up? It is believing correctly, behaving as God desires, remembering that I am at peace with him through Christ, trusting his promises and looking forward to heaven. It is, in short, filling my mind with thoughts of what God has revealed in his Word. To stand firm in battle, I must feed my mind. It must be nourished by divine truth. To stand against the enemy, I must feed my mind. I must see things as God sees them. The battle is for the mind — for mine, as well as for everybody else's. But

God's armour is more than enough. There is no need to be overcome by any of the evil forces that threaten to crush us.

We should think, rather, in terms of advance

In addition to the armour which perfectly protects us, God has given us two weapons to attack with. It is not enough to remain on the defensive. It is not sufficient to hold our ground. We must invade and capture the enemy's territory. We must go forward.

Our first attacking weapon is the *sword* — **'the sword of the Spirit, which is the word of God'** (6:17). The hands which hold it are ours, but strong invisible hands are placed over them. We wield the sword as best we can, but it is the invisible hands which give it force, direction and cutting power. God's work is not done without us. It is none the less God's Spirit who does God's work.

The Spirit's sword is the Word of God. How are the devil and his agents brought to release their grip on the minds they have captured? How are error and ungodliness put to flight? How are people brought to submit to Christ? How are victories won in the spiritual dimension? How are we to advance?

Signs and wonders will not do it. Nor will clever arguments. All God's work is done by God's Word; and what is not done by God's Word is not God's work. The devil cannot stand against the Holy Spirit working through the Scriptures. It is by the proclamation of God's Word that minds are enlightened, lives are changed, and conversions take place. Spiritual work is done by spiritual weaponry. This is obvious, but we need to be reminded of it. The declaration of the Bible's message must always be our great priority. There is no true spiritual advance where the Bible does not lead the way. The Holy Spirit has no other sword apart from the book which he has inspired. Those who believe this will give themselves to spreading the biblical message. What happens on the battlefield will not disappoint them.

But God has also given us a second attacking weapon (6:18-20). As Paul talks about it his Roman soldier fades from view, for this spiritual weapon has no earthly equivalent. We have a secret weapon which has no human parallel. It is *prayer*.

Our armour must be worn, and our sword wielded, in a spirit of prayer. There are many sorts of prayer at our disposal and we are to use them all (6:18). We are to let the Spirit lead us in this, and we are never to stop. Our prayer life is never to become sleepy or intermittent, and we are to intercede for all believers everywhere. We cannot wage successful spiritual warfare without becoming prayer experts.

There are some people for whom we should be particularly careful to pray (6:19-20). They are gospel preachers. It is for this reason that Paul asks his readers to pray in a special way for him. As he uses the Spirit's sword, he needs to be able to speak as he should. The gospel requires bold proclamation. The 'mystery' which it reveals (and of which he has spoken at length in chapter 3) is open to misunderstanding, and needs to be made very clear indeed. It is his preaching of the gospel which has landed him in prison, and there is always the temptation to soft-pedal its message in order to avoid even worse suffering. So they must pray that he may be as bold as ever. No other sort of ministry will do.

Gospel preachers are not supermen. Left to themselves, they are unable to persuade men and women to believe the message, and they certainly cannot present that message both boldly and fittingly. Without God's help, they are nothing. It is essential that believers everywhere storm heaven's gates and beseech God to accompany such preachers in a remarkable way. Prayer thrives where those who pray know as much as possible about the preachers for whom they are interceding. This is why Paul has sent Tychicus to the Ephesians (6:21-22). This exemplary Christian worker will tell them in detail about Paul's present situation, which will also prove to be a considerable source of encouragement to them. We pray for those with whom we have a sense of fellowship. That sense of fellowship is greatly strengthened when we have personal news of them.

Paul, then, has not left us in any doubt. The gospel will advance in this world if we will but use the weapons God has given us. We need to proclaim the Word of God and pray. This must not be done in fits and starts, but with constancy and determination. This is the way forward. This is the way which God pledges to bless. Who will go that way?

The difference between real soldiers and part-time ones is that real soldiers use their weapons. It is not enough to clean weapons, to use them in drill and to generally admire them. They must be turned on the enemy! Not until then can we even begin to imagine what is their true power.

Who will take the Word to the unconverted? Who will let it loose in this darkened world? Who will preach, or print, or write to others, or speak to them personally? Who will gather boys and girls, to tell them the gospel? Who will give out biblical tracts? What will you do to bring rebellious thoughts into capitivity to Christ?

Who will pray for those who spread the Word? Who will intercede for gospel preachers nearby and across the world? Who will do it every day, and several times a day? Who will implore God to bless Sunday School teachers, youth leaders, home visitors and all personal witnesses? We need to advance. Holding our ground is not enough. There is territory everywhere waiting to be snatched from enemy control. It can be captured — it really can — if we will do things God's way.

And so Paul comes to the end of his magnificent letter. He does so in the same spirit as he opened it (6:23-24). His love for his readers is as obvious as ever. His desire is that God the Father and the Lord Jesus Christ may grant that their faith should be accompanied by peace and love. And what he wants for them, he wants for all Christians. He prays that God will strengthen and bless all who love his Son with an incorruptible love.

Do *you* love the Lord Jesus Christ, so wondrously unveiled in the Epistle to the Ephesians, and especially in its first three chapters? Will you live for him in the church, in the world, and at home — even if every single day is a difficult battle?